THE ENGLISH BOROUGH AND ROYAL ADMINISTRATION

THE ENGLISH BOROUGH AND ROYAL
ADMINISTRATION, 1130-1307

Charles R. Young

DUKE UNIVERSITY PRESS · DURHAM, N. C. · 1961

To my wife, Betty

This book is published with the assistance of a grant to the Duke University Press by the Ford Foundation.

PREFACE

My interest in the study of boroughs began when Professor Carl Stephenson suggested an investigation of English boroughs and royal administration as one of several possible topics for a dissertation. Having adopted his suggestion, I attempted to plunge headlong into the reading of twelfth-century pipe rolls, only to find my unfamiliarity with exchequer procedure almost as much a barrier to my understanding of these records as was the "record type" in the early printed volumes. Since that first naïve approach and the subsequent background study that proved necessary, this investigation has been the source of continual education for me as it led through the maze of twelfth- and thirteenth-century administrative history. The resulting manuscript has alternately expanded as additional aspects needing study were encountered and contracted as more perspective made possible the consolidation or elimination of superfluous material. My principal regret is that Professor Stephenson did not live to see even the first draft of the book as it emerged from the embryo of the original dissertation, or to give the manuscript the benefit of his advice and criticism, which he had so generously offered.

In this book I have attempted to deal with the essentials of the administrative responsibilities undertaken by English boroughs, while sternly resisting the temptation to pursue the many subsidiary issues suggested by the evidence. Although the illustrations of administrative activity taken from contemporary records are intended to show something of the large amount of such activity and the rich variety within general types of activity, for each illustration used many more had to be rejected, even at the risk of failing to follow all the intricacies of the administrative pattern they seem to reflect. Perhaps the reader will find a kind of recognition among some of the examples chosen that will enable him to supply something of the very human stories that give interest to administrative study, but that had to be excluded from the final product in order not to obscure the main lines of administrative responsibilities.

Quite misleading as a visual image is the impression often given of the medieval English borough as a kind of island estranged from the main flow of governmental activity and the society around it. A more accurate image would be that of the borough as a part of an organism in touch with the other parts of English government and in close contact with the royal administration at the center. This book deals with that relationship between the English borough and the royal administration from 1130 to 1307, a formative period for both institutions. By the latter date the borough had become indispensable as a unit of royal administration for the local level in spite of grants of liberties and immunities to boroughs during the same period. Such grants placed the borough and its officials in direct contact with the royal government by the transfer to burgesses and their officials of the responsibilities formerly borne by sheriffs and other royal officials. Whether the borough officials were elective or royal appointees, whether the borough they served was rich and powerful or not, the king's authority was superior, and all alike served him in the administrative system.

The activity resulting from this relationship is analyzed and discussed in chapters that deal with financial responsibilities, administration of justice, military and naval responsibilities, regulation of commerce, and miscellaneous responsibilities. In final perspective, it becomes clear that the boroughs were especially important in all areas concerned with finance and commerce, as the kings and royal ministers worked out ways to turn the growing wealth of the towns to royal advantage.

In writing this book, I have become increasingly aware of my indebtedness to friends and colleagues. I should particularly like to express the appreciation that I feel for the interest shown by the late Professor Sidney Painter of The Johns Hopkins University, whose criticism of an earlier draft and discussion of that draft with me were invaluable. Professors John R. Alden and Harold T. Parker of Duke University provided encouragement when it was most needed. Professor Bryce D. Lyon of the University of California (Berkeley) accepted the arduous task of reading the final draft, and his suggestions that I have been able to incorporate have improved the book. Mr. Emerson Ford of the Duke University Library patiently and efficiently handled my requests for books from other libraries. My wife, whose expertness in typing extends to spotting mistakes of many kinds, has helped me throughout. It is too much to hope that such assistance has prevented all errors, and for those that remain the responsibility must be wholly mine.

Not the least of my obligations is to the Duke University Council on Research which provided a subsidy making publication of this book possible.

Charles R. Young

CONTENTS

ABBREVIATIONS USED IN THE FOOTNOTES

B.B.C.   *British Borough Charters 1042-1660.* Vol. I, ed. A. Ballard, Vol. II, ed. J. Tait. Cambridge, 1913-43.

C.C.R.   *Calendar of the Close Rolls 1272-1307.* London, 1900-1908.

C.L.R.   *Calendar of the Liberate Rolls 1227-1251.* London, 1916-30.

C.P.R.   *Calendar of the Patent Rolls 1232-1307.* London, 1893-1913.

C.R.   *Close Rolls 1227-1272.* London, 1902-38.

P.R.   *Pipe Roll.*

    31 Henry I.   Facsimile of the 1833 Record Commission ed. London, 1929.

    2-4 Henry II.   Facsimile of the 1844 Record Commission ed. London, 1930.

    5 Henry II (and following years). Pipe Roll Society. London 1884-1955.

    1 Richard I.   Record Commission. London, 1844.

Pat.R.   *Patent Rolls 1216-1232.* London, 1901-3.

Rot.Litt.Cl.   *Rotuli Litterarum Clausarum.* Record Commission. London, 1833-44.

Rot.Litt.Pat.   *Rotuli Litterarum Patentium.* Record Commission. London, 1835.

ABBREVIATIONS USED IN THE FOOTNOTES

THE ENGLISH BOROUGH AND ROYAL ADMINISTRATION

CHAPTER I. INTRODUCTION

THE study of boroughs as privileged town communities
has attracted the interest of medieval historians, who have
produced works on this subject noted for depth of learning
but not free of scholarly controversy. These historians have attempted to trace the appearance of the borough community to
the very moment of conception and, from that point, the development of some kind of self-government within that community. Since the list of scholars who have contributed to our
understanding of the borough includes William Stubbs, F. W.
Maitland, J. H. Round, Mary Bateson, Charles Gross, and
(more recently) James Tait and Carl Stephenson, to name
a few, it is with some trepidation that another study in this
field is offered. This is especially true of one on a fairly broad
scope rather than the detailed, logical analysis almost typical
of books dealing with the borough. But further examination
will show that another general characteristic of these books is
that there is a concentration by most scholars upon the internal
functioning of the borough, usually treated in isolation from
other parts of the realm. Only Erwin Meyer in the chapter he
contributed to *The English Government at Work, 1327-1336*

has demonstrated the possibilities of another approach, which views the borough as a unit in a larger institutional network and examines the relation between the borough and the royal administration at the center of that network.[1] His work has been the inspiration for this present study.

An application of Meyer's methods to the records of the twelfth and thirteenth centuries shows that his conclusions have a much wider application than he made of them, and that the responsibilities of boroughs to the royal administration already existed in an earlier period, when neither the borough nor the royal administration had reached the fully developed organization of the fourteenth century. Extension of the chronological limits makes possible answers to other questions, such as whether during the course of the thirteenth century (when we have comparable chancery records) there was any increase or decrease in administrative responsibilities for the boroughs, and this extension also provides some opportunity to make quantitative judgments as to the importance of these responsibilities to the royal administration over a long period of time. Furthermore, the unique value of the English records is fully utilized only when a subject is pursued year after year through the consecutive documents, which tend to correct the interpretation suggested by a single instance and to supplement each other by illustrating all the facets of a particular responsibility. To a great extent the impression of such responsibilities is conveyed only by the total quantity of evidence available and the tremendous variety of administrative activity that this evidence contains.

The picture of borough development that emerges from this mass of detail is that of burgesses being given more and more administrative responsibilities. Therefore, the emphasis

1. Erwin F. Meyer in James F. Willard *et al., The English Government at Work, 1327-1336* (Cambridge, Mass., 1940-50), III, 105-141.

often placed upon a development toward independence from the royal administration or even the attainment of autonomy by the boroughs appears to have been misplaced. It is true that the privileges and immunities of the borough do increase during the later twelfth and thirteenth centuries, but inseparable from these privileges is the need for the burgesses or their officials to assume the functions formerly performed by the sheriff or other royal officials. With the pattern of increasing administrative responsibilities for boroughs thus established, the precedent was followed, and the expanding activities of the central administration were made effective in the local community of the borough by assigning even further responsibilities to the burgesses. Sometimes they resisted, showing an awareness of the trend, but there is little evidence that such resistance was successful in staving off new responsibilities. The result is that the boroughs for all their privileges were more integrally a part of the royal administration in its elaborated form by 1307 than they had been in the laissez-faire days of 1130. What had begun as haphazard experiments in the use of burgesses had become regularized by the close of Edward I's reign, sometimes by statutes in parliament, itself an institution drawing the boroughs into new connections with the king.

For the limited consideration of developments within the borough that is necessary to understanding the place of the borough in royal administration, the main problem is that of controversial interpretation among the views of historians, who have devoted much attention to this subject since 1726, when the earliest work still worth reading was published. Charles Gross's assessment of that work by Thomas Madox, in spite of the early date, as being a "storehouse" of information written by a "painstaking and truth-loving scholar" still stands.[2] Al-

2. Charles Gross, *A Bibliography of British Municipal History* (Harvard Historical Studies: V, N. Y., 1897), p. xxv.

though the author was primarily interested in the *firma burgi,* the implications of his study led him to the general subject of the development of the borough community, and his intimate knowledge of the records of chancery and exchequer, illustrated by copious extracts from records, in some cases yet unpublished elsewhere, makes his book a starting point for the researcher.[3] The meaning of the *firma burgi* privilege for the borough community was further elaborated by William Stubbs, and his views on this subject are useful, although many of his ideas about the borough have been superseded. Charles Gross made an important contribution to the study of boroughs by his discussion of the relationship between the guild merchant and the government of the borough. Fundamental books on the internal development of the borough were published more recently by James Tait and Carl Stephenson.[4]

However, it was F. W. Maitland, in a dictum laid down for the future historian of the borough, who recognized more fully the broader implications in the development of the borough community:

He [the future historian of the borough] will, so we think, consider the borough from two different points of view, and indeed, were this possible, he should occupy both at the same time; for the borough is both organ and organism. On the one hand, we have here a piece of England which is governed in a somewhat peculiar way. To use our modern terms, there is within it a "local authority" of a somewhat unusual type and there is more "local self-government" here than elsewhere. On the other hand, we have here a community which differs from the other communities of the land in that it is attaining the degree and kind of organization which we call corporate, so that, for example, it will be capable of ap-

3. Thomas Madox, *Firma Burgi, or an Historical Essay Concerning the Cities Towns and Buroughs of England* (London, 1726).
4. William Stubbs, *The Constitutional History of England* (5th ed.; Oxford, 1891); Charles Gross, *The Gild Merchant* (Oxford, 1890); James Tait, *The Medieval English Borough* (Manchester, 1936); Carl Stephenson, *Borough and Town* (Cambridge, Mass., 1933).

pearing as an individual landowner among individual landowners, as a single wrong-doer. Neither point of view should be neglected.[5]

As Maitland understood the problem, the burgesses formed a group of franchise holders and were subject to royal rules like other franchise holders; their privileges might be lost either by abuse or by failure to claim them before the justices on eyre. Maitland never worked out his ideas in detail, but his suggestion might well serve as a guide to anyone studying the borough today.

Yet, in spite of all that has been written about the borough, the problem of its relations to the royal administration has not yet received due attention from historians. No comprehensive studies have been published dealing with this subject for the twelfth and thirteenth centuries, and no writer has carried out Maitland's dictum. Such a stimulating book as J. E. A. Jolliffe's *Angevin Kingship* underlines the need for a study in this area, for, even though Jolliffe demonstrates the general dependence of the Angevin kings upon their bailiffs and places considerable emphasis upon the interaction between the itinerant king and local bailiffs who made up the network of administration, he completely ignores the importance of the borough and its officials as a part of this network.[6] However, there has been much specialized work on subjects that fall within the scope of this general problem and that can most conveniently be discussed in relation to the topics with which they are concerned. For example, the pioneer work by Madox on the *firma burgi,* the more recent treatment of that subject by Tait, and Stephenson's research on borough aids and the development of borough taxation will be considered in later chapters.

5. Frederick Pollock and Frederic William Maitland, *The History of English Law before the Time of Edward I* (2nd ed.; Cambridge, 1923), I, 635.
6. J. E. A. Jolliffe, *Angevin Kingship* (New York, 1955).

Clearly most of the information about the place of the borough in royal administration must come directly from the sources—mainly the records of the exchequer and the chancery. In fact, the pipe roll for 1129-30 and the continuous series in print from the years 1155 through 1212 provide the most valuable evidence for the twelfth century. Among the chancery records, both the close and patent rolls are printed in full or in calendar for the entire period of the thirteenth century. Borough charters have been analyzed in a separate publication, making reference to the charter rolls unnecessary. Unfortunately, the *liberate* rolls after 1260 have not been printed, but this deficiency is mostly significant in affecting some quantitative judgments on the scope of administrative activities. It is probable that documents not available in print would reinforce rather than produce any fundamental change in the conclusions based on evidence from the printed records.

Secondary works provide little detailed guidance in the use of these sources for the subject of the borough and royal administration, although general statements upon such administrative responsibilities are frequently made, and it has long been recognized that burgesses had such responsibilities. The emphasis mainly upon the internal development of the borough community shows that by the early twelfth century the borough was already being treated by the royal administration as a community different from the other units of local administration. This development made it possible for borough officials to assume many of the local administrative responsibilities from royal officials, and grants of immunities to boroughs made it necessary for them to do so. The burgesses, from the point of view of the royal administration, were franchise holders responsibile for certain administrative functions and liable, collectively or individually, for the execution of those functions. While these developments were occurring within the borough, the royal administration was becoming a specialized and well-organized system with records preserved by the practice of enrolment. These records provide the main sources used in succeeding chapters. Unfortunately, neither these nor other contemporary sources are very informative in regard to the preliminary question about the royal authority for using burgesses and borough officials for a bewildering variety of administrative tasks during the period from 1130 to 1307.

CHAPTER II. ROYAL AUTHORITY AND BOROUGH OFFICIALS

THE administrative tasks performed by burgesses in the twelfth and thirteenth centuries show a practical recognition of royal authority over the boroughs, but almost nothing can be found that serves as a general statement of the basis for this authority. Even the legal writers of this period were little given to abstract theorizing and less concerned with the borough as a part of the realm worthy of their attention. As for the burgesses themselves, they seem to have accepted the king's authority without question except when royal orders encroached upon some liberty granted by their charter. This exception, this jealous insistence upon the exercise of every liberty included in the borough charter, provides the key to understanding the relationship of royal authority to the boroughs.

Boroughs as they appear in Domesday Book with few exceptions demonstrate none of the qualities of privileged communities, but are treated as administrative units subordinated to royal authority in the same way as the surrounding country.[1]

1. Stephenson, *Borough and Town*, p. 120.

Emancipation from this completely dependent status came about only gradually during the course of the next century and a half through the process of obtaining charters granting special liberties to boroughs. It is in regard to this process that Bracton came closest to discussing the question of royal authority and the boroughs. In his discussion of such charters he first expressed the broad powers of the king: "And it is to be known that the lord king himself, who has ordinary jurisdiction and dignity, and power over all who are in his realm, truly has in his hand all rights which pertain to the crown and the lay power and the material sword, [and] which pertain to the government of the realm. . . ."[2] Next he specifically listed justice and judgment and the attributes of preserving peace among these rights. However, the king could transfer such privileges to private persons. Bracton's next statement is particularly illuminating: "For it ought to be clear to every person that things of this kind pertain to the crown, unless there be some one who can show the contrary from some special favor received."[3] That these statements would apply to a borough is clearly indicated when he continues by discussing the problem involved when there arose an apparent conflict of the privileges granted and chooses for his illustration the grant of a fair or market to citizens or burgesses. The conflict was resolved by producing the charters to establish priority of one over the other.[4] These passages in Bracton leave no doubt that he regarded the royal authority as unquestionable except in cases where privileges had been granted to private persons, and that one method of proving such a grant was to produce the charter containing the privilege in question.

The effect of such principles upon the status of the borough

2. Henricus de Bracton, *De Legibus et Consuetudinibus Angliae,* ed. George E. Woodbine (New Haven, 1915-42), I, 166.
3. *Ibid.,* I, 167.
4. *Ibid.,* I, 169-173.

was not overlooked by Maitland, who found a correlation with the attitudes implied in the charters themselves. He pointed out that the charters represent the king as giving a gift to the burgesses and their heirs, that the group of burgesses is primarily a franchise holder, and that the king continued to exercise his authority because he could and did revoke this franchise if the burgesses exceeded the powers granted from above.[5] The discussion by Mr. J. E. A. Jolliffe of why royal officials obeyed the Angevin monarchy and what happened when they did not obey applies also to the measures of control exercised over the boroughs. Because Henry II met the difficulty of securing obedience by his choice of men to serve him rather than by any general measures, any particular order might require special sanctions to insure that it was obeyed. Sometimes such sanctions would include a threat either against the officials or the communities they served. As Jolliffe comments, "Disseizin *per voluntatem* was at all times the royal discipline of which the Crown's servants had most reason to stand in awe, and that which was used with most decisive effect."[6] The records of both exchequer and chancery bear witness to the frequent and often capricious use of this power to take away the liberties of a borough and seize it into the king's hands. Jolliffe, in another connection, cites a letter patent of King John to the bailiffs of the ports to illustrate his contention that the threat of force never lay far beneath the surface relationships: "This is the ultimate threat upon which for the most part rests the obedience of the King's servants and the orderly conduct of the realm. 'If our business fail through your default,' writes John to his bailiffs, '*nos inde capiemus ad vos sicut ad inimicos nostros.*' "[7]

Some idea of the process of enforcing royal authority in

5. Pollock and Maitland, *History of English Law*, I, 668, 673, 688.
6. Jolliffe, *Angevin Kingship*, pp. 61-65.
7. *Ibid.*, p. 99.

the boroughs of the thirteenth century can be found in the following contemporary references. In one case from 1254 the king forced the mayor and citizens of London to appear in court to answer because a prisoner had escaped from the jail at Newgate. The Londoners replied that custody of the jail belonged to the sheriffs and denied responsibility for the actions of those officials on the grounds that, although they elected the sheriffs, the king's approval was required before they could perform their official duties. The sheriffs were arrested and later released on surety of the mayor, but the king would not allow them to remain in office and a new election had to be held.[8] Four years later a royal inquisition was held into the performance of London officials who were rumored not holding the city in faithful custody and, in consequence, the king's council deposed the mayor, sheriffs, and alderman from office.[9] The superior power of the crown is shown even more clearly in an instance from 1285 when the mayor of London was cited to appear before royal justices. He resigned his office and handed the seal of the city over to the aldermen before answering with the claim that the liberties of London provided that such an inquisition could not be held without forty days' notice. Provoked by this claim, the royal treasurer seized the mayoralty and the liberties of London into the king's hand, and the city continued to be administered by keepers until 1298.[10] In other disputes the king had shown that he might proceed either against the individual mayor or the city as a whole.[11] Usually the Londoners would offer a sum

8. *De Antiquis Legibus Liber. Cronica Maiorum et Vicecomitum Londoninarum,* ed. Thomas Stapleton (Camden Society, No. XXXIV: London, 1846), p. 22. Hereinafter cited as *Cronica Maiorum et Vicecomitum Londoninarum.* This chronicle has been translated by Henry T. Riley, *Chronicles of the Mayors and Sheriffs of London, A.D. 1188 to A.D. 1274* (London, 1863).

9. William Stubbs, ed., *Chronicles of the Reigns of Edward I and Edward II* (Rolls Series: London, 1882-83), I, 49-50 (*Annales Londoniensis*).

10. *Ibid.,* pp. 94-95, 102.

11. *Cronica Maiorum et Vicecomitum Londoninarum,* pp. 8, 14.

of money as a fine in order to placate the king and regain their liberties.[12]

Other references illustrate the procedure of producing a charter to demonstrate the validity of privileges which had been called into question. In this way in a case from the time of King John, the citizens of Lincoln sustained the argument that they did not have to plead outside their walls and the bailiffs of Dunwich referred to their charter in 1225 to prove they did not have to answer outside their walls except before the itinerant justices.[13] On the other hand, in a case of 1292 when the mayor and community of Carlisle, unable to produce a charter of Henry II which they said had been burned, did not wish to have the chancery records searched, their liberties were seized into the king's hand and he named a keeper for the borough.[14] Similarly the claim of the citizens of York to hold the wapentake of Anesty was not allowed when an erasure in the date was found in the charter of King John which they produced, and when the record failed to specify that area in the entry concerning the grant of York to the citizens in fee farm.[15]

The assertion of royal authority is made quite explicit in some cases where the liberties being claimed by boroughs seem to encroach upon it. When the bailiffs of Southampton failed to produce a man wanted in a royal court, the sheriff was ordered to produce him notwithstanding the liberties of Southampton, with the advisory notice added that "he should know that the burgesses of Southampton have no liberty such that he should not carry out the command of the lord king. And therefore he should not omit to execute the command of

---

12. *The Memoranda Roll for . . . the First Year of the Reign of King John (1199-1200)* (Pipe Roll Society, n.s. 21, London, 1943), p. 8.

13. *Curia Regis Rolls* (London, 1922-57), I, 293; XII, 68.

14. *Placita de Quo Warranto* (Rec. Comm., London, 1818), p. 121a.

15. G. O. Sayles, *Select Cases in the Court of King's Bench under Edward I* (Selden Society 55, 57-58, London, 1936-39), I, 62. There is a reference to this case in *Rotuli Hundredorum* (Rec. Comm., London, 1812-18), I, 126.

the lord king, so that he himself will not be seized."[16] In 1281 three men and the mayor of Sandwich were accused of mistreating a messenger carrying a royal writ. They made the defense that they had to answer only at the court of Shepway, but this was disallowed with the statement that neither the barons of the Cinque Ports nor anyone else in the realm could claim such a liberty that they would not have to respond concerning contempt done the king wherever he commanded. Not only were the defendants convicted and jailed, but it was also decided that because the mayor was involved Sandwich should lose its liberties.[17] Serious as such loss was to a borough, there are many illustrations to show that the loss was not irretrievable provided the burgesses were able to pay a fine or an increment to their farm when it was restored.[18] The bailiffs of Worcester were unable to sustain the claim that a royal writ of novel disseisin could not be impleaded within their town, even though they explained that disseisin was dealt with in their guildhall in cases where violent ejections from the property had occurred within the last forty days. The royal justices before whom the bailiffs appeared held that because they were unable to show a charter or recognition by a royal court of the privilege claimed, although admitting that they themselves could redress the use of fresh force, maintained that it was not right that the king by his writs should be of lower estate than the bailiffs of the town without the king's writ, and, therefore, that the defendant must answer the royal writ in regard to the disseisin.[19]

16. *Curia Regis Rolls,* XI, 363.

17. *Placitorum in Domo Capitulari Westmonasteriensi Asservatorum Abbreviatio* (Rec. Comm., London, 1818), p. 273a. The man involved as mayor of Sandwich in this case had opposed royal officials to the point of an armed resistance and siege in 1275. At that time he was bailiff of the town. See Sayles, *Select Cases . . . King's Bench,* I, 13-14.

18. E.g., see *Rotulorum Originalium in Curia Scaccarii Abbreviatio* (Rec. Comm., London, 1805), pp. 7, 26, 47, 49.

19. Sayles, *Select Cases . . . King's Bench,* III, 37.

This question of the status of the borough in relation to the royal government has been admirably summarized by Mr. B. Wilkinson:

For the most part, the borough could judge, collect the king's dues, and keep the king's peace; but for the townsmen themselves this was no better than a negative safeguard, an immunity. It was the privilege of doing for the king what he did not find it expedient to do for himself.

To the ruler, the town governments were royal instruments. Boroughs were only towns given that title by virtue of a royal charter or summons to parliament; in their first beginnings they had been primarily royal centres of administration and defence. Nor did either boroughs or cities ever lose this essential quality.[20]

The most fundamental privilege obtained by charter from the king was the right of the burgesses themselves to collect the farm of the borough and account for it at the exchequer. These grants of the *firma burgi* privilege to Lincoln by 1130 and London in 1131 followed by numerous grants to other boroughs later in the century provide clear illustrations of Mr. Wilkinson's statement on the nature of borough privileges, involving an immunity on the one hand and the use of town governments as royal instruments to supersede the sheriff in collecting the borough farm on the other. Maitland explained the legal results of this grant and emphasized that the king did not give up his rights as landlord to the borough community. Each burgess continued to hold his tenement from the king directly or from some other person, for no tenements were held from the borough community. As part of the proof that the *firma burgi* privilege did not imply a kind of corporate ownership of land within the borough, Maitland pointed out that even with the *firma burgi* a borough community did

20. B. Wilkinson, *The Constitutional History of England 1216-1399* (London, Toronto, and N. Y., 1948-58), III, 194-195.

not profit from an escheat within the borough. Maitland summarized his discussion of the *firma burgi* in these words:

The general theory of the law seems to be that, in becoming a farmer, the burgesses become rather a bailiff than a tenant, though a bailiff who, like many other medieval bailiffs, has to account each year for a fixed sum and may make a profit or a loss out of his office.[21]

With the spread of the *firma burgi* privilege, an important part of the local administrative responsibilities rested with borough officials; thus the sheriffs were enabled to concentrate their efforts on administration of the county and the collection of certain revenues outside the borough farm. Something of the scope of the duties assumed by borough officials can be seen from the appearances of the bailiff of Kingston at the exchequer as reconstructed from various exchequer records of the late thirteenth century by Miss Mabel Mills. The names of all those accounting at the exchequer were entered on the memoranda rolls in the section entitled *Adventus Vicecomitum*. Miss Mills found that the sheriff of Surrey and Sussex was ordered to appear at the exchequer for audit of his account on Monday, January 31, 1295, and that he was accompanied by officials who represented the various "liberties" within the two counties. The bailiff of Kingston was one of these officials, and at this session he was the last to be heard. He had withdrawn from the exchequer without license from the treasurer and the barons, and the sheriff was ordered to distrain him. The first proffer of the account later in the year shows clearly the separate responsibility of the Kingston bailiff. Although the exchequer term began on Monday, April 11, and the sheriff made his payments into the receipts on Thursday of that week, the bailiff of Kingston did not make his payments until April 26. At the second proffer of that year, the sheriff appeared on October 7,

21. Pollock and Maitland, *History of English Law*, I, 651.

and the free men of Kingston were represented by a new bailiff, who rendered their account.[22] During this year the bailiff of Kingston was charged with the borough farm and its increase, with an annual rent from land managed by the men of Kingston for the king, and with the annual rent from purprestures and serjeanties taken over from the sheriff in 1280. He also had collected some returns of a temporary nature from summonses of the pipe and from summonses of the green wax.[23]

Borough officials whose duty it was to answer at the exchequer for the borough farm were held strictly accountable by the barons, as illustrated especially by entries in the memoranda rolls. The roll of 1199-1200 notes that the men of Colchester failed to appear, although they had been summoned.[24] The burgesses of Canterbury left without making a settlement about their payment for having their town and other liberties, and the sheriff was ordered to draw up a list of names. This list as entered in the margin includes eleven names of burgesses who should appear at the exchequer and submit to justice for their offense.[25] Even more illuminating is the case of the men of Ipswich who failed to account for having their liberties and for an amercement, or to send anyone to account for them. The barons of the exchequer ordered them to be put upon the account of the sheriff, but they retained the farm by making a payment for this privilege.[26] References in the roll for 1230-31 show the men of Kingston, Huntingdon, and Bedford

22. [M. H. Mills], *The Pipe Roll for 1295 Surrey Membrane* (Surrey Record Society, VII, Guildford and Esher, 1924), pp. xi, xiv, xvi-xix. This account is based primarily on unpublished memoranda rolls. The status of Kingston as a borough even though its citizens were always referred to as the "free men of Kingston" was affirmed by James Tait in *B.B.C.*, II, xx-xxi.

23. Mills, pp. 2 ff., xlviii-li.

24. *Memoranda Roll I John (1199-1200)*, p. 82.

25. *Ibid.*, pp. 31-32.

26. *Ibid.*, pp. 77, 79. The *P.R. 1 John*, p. 265 records payment of 60 m. "pro habendis libertatibus suis." This is given more clearly in *P.R. 2 John*, p. 148 as "Burgenses de Gipeswiz debent c m. pro habenda carte R. de uilla sua habenda ad firmam computatis lx m." The charter of 1200 includes the *firma burgi* privileges; see *B.B.C.*, I, 226.

and the reeves of Nottingham and Derby all imprisoned for delinquencies in payments.[27] That same year the sheriff was ordered to produce the bailiffs and reeves and twelve of the better men of Norwich to answer for their debts, and Peter, the reeve of Ipswich, had to put up security that he would pay by a specified time or return to prison with four of the better men.[28]

An early student of borough history, Thomas Madox, gave the definitive answer to this question of the liability of the boroughs and their officials who had the duty of answering for their farm at the exchequer:

By the Ancient and settled Course of the Exchequer, the Sheriffs of Towns, the Bailifs, or other Officers who accounted to the King for the Ferme of their Town or other Duties, were answerable to the King in their Own Persons lands and chatells upon their Accompt, or for Defaults and Contempts in Accounting.[29]

If the bailiff were insolvent, the king was at liberty to require the borough farm from the borough itself. Usually, this meant that the king would take the farm into his own hands and collect the revenues by means of an official appointed as *custos,* but the debt might be levied on the burgesses individually, or at least on the wealthier men among them.[30] In spite of the burden involved in the possession of the *firma burgi,* English burgesses were willing to pay the king well for this privilege because it gave them much greater freedom from exactions by the sheriff.[31]

In referring to the *firma burgi* privilege, which was fundamental for the use of a borough by the officials of the royal

27. *The Memoranda Roll of the King's Remembrancer for Michaelmas 1230-Trinity 1231,* ed. Chalfant Robinson (Pipe Roll Soc., n.s., XI, Princeton, 1933), pp. 4-5, 8, 9, 63.
28. *Ibid.,* pp. 26, 27.
29. Madox, *Firma Burgi,* p. 161; see the estimate of Madox's contribution in Frederic William Maitland, *Township and Borough* (Cambridge, 1898), p. 77.
30. Madox, pp. 164, 181, 232.
31. Many such entries occur in the pipe rolls. For example, *P.R. 3 Ric. I,* p. 109: "Burgenses de Bedeford' r.c. de quater xx m. pro habenda uilla sua ad feodi firmam et pro habendis libertatibus suis secundum cartam suam."

administration, the burgesses as a group are usually said to have the privilege, but the personal instruments by which this responsibility and other royal administrative orders were executed were the borough officials, whether called reeves, bailiffs, mayors, or some other title. This distinction between the burgesses and borough officials becomes significant for the thirteenth century in view of the fact that chancery writs were often addressed to the officials of the borough only. This raises the question whether such officials in any given case were simply acting as royal agents in the borough, as the sheriff acted in the county, or whether they acted as the agent of the burgesses upon whom the obligation fell.

Of the various names for borough officials, that of reeve (*prepositus*) causes little practical difficulty in understanding chancery enrolments. This title, common in the pipe rolls of the twelfth century, is found at first interchangeably with that of bailiff (*ballivus*) in the thirteenth, and later seems to have been replaced by that term.[32] The word mayor applied to an officer, nearly always elective, who undoubtedly acted directly in place of the burgesses as a whole. It is less often stressed that the mayor also represented the king's interests, as Mr. J. E. A. Jolliffe has pointed out in discussing this office:

It embodied in itself both the elective right of the community and the royal commission, so that the king appointed a mayor to York *tamquam ballivus noster et major vester,* and, being added to the court of aldermen or jurats, it represented the town to the outside world.[33]

The many administrative orders addressed to mayors prove that in practice, as well as in theory, the king regarded the mayor as his official to command at will. The real difficulty lies,

32. My own observation agrees with the opinion of Stephenson, *Borough and Town,* p. 174.
33. J. E. A. Jolliffe, *The Constitutional History of Medieval England* (London, 1937), p. 322.

then, in the meaning of the term "bailiff" as used in the chancery writs, and the degree of responsibility for the burgesses that it implies. Even here there is no doubt that the burgesses were directly involved in the administrative responsibilities given in writs addressed to the bailiffs and proved men of a borough, to the mayor and bailiffs, or to the barons and bailiffs of one of the Cinque Ports.

In some cases where the burgesses had obtained the right to elect their own officials, reference to the charters quickly shows that the bailiffs acted for the burgesses, but the surprising feature of most charters is the absence of such a privilege.[34] Adolphus Ballard explained this omission by concluding that the grant of *firma burgi* implied the right to elect borough officials, necessary for collecting and answering for the borough farm, and that any separate statement of the right of election was therefore superfluous. Furthermore, Ballard pointed out that King John addressed writs to "mayors" in nine boroughs, in spite of the fact that there are no known charter provisions for this office in these places, an action that shows that charters did not always fully reflect usage.[35]

This explanation was challenged by Carl Stephenson, who held that the two privileges, *firma burgi* and elective borough officials, were separate. The presumption that the rights were independent is raised by showing that the known grants of *firma burgi* were about twice those of election, and that this holds true even when chancery enrolment of the thirteenth century practically rules out the possibility of lost charters. Moreover, this presumption is borne out by direct evidence from the pipe rolls for five boroughs showing that farming preceded election in one case and that the reverse was true in the other cases.[36]

34. Tait in *B.B.C.*, II, lvi-lvii.
35. *Ibid.*, I, lxxxvi-lxxxvii.
36. Stephenson, *Borough and Town*, pp. 167-170.

The conclusions of Stephenson, in turn, were subjected to critical appraisal by James Tait. He was able to show that Stephenson had overlooked a pipe roll reference in one case and had been misled by current misdating of a charter in another. In other cases, Tait uses the same evidence to reach opposite conclusions, providing an incidental illustration of how ambiguous the evidence of the pipe rolls is for this problem. He added four cases which he thought provided evidence that the right of election necessarily followed from the right of *firma burgi*. At Dublin in 1215 the citizens were enfeoffed with the reeveship when they got the *firma burgi,* and the Nottingham charter of 1189 contains no other reference to the *firma burgi* than that in the grant allowing the burgesses to choose the reeve "to answer for the king's farm and to pay it directly into the exchequer," although they accounted for the farm at the exchequer. Oxford is known to have been choosing bailiffs about 1257 with no authorization by charter unless it was the fee farm granted in 1199. The answer to a writ of *quo warranto* at Liverpool in 1292 seems also to show a direct relationship of the two privileges.[37]

Faced with such contradictory arguments, it is difficult to draw any very trustworthy conclusions, but Ballard and Tait seem to have the balance in their favor. Stephenson's conclusions rest mainly upon inferences from the pipe rolls that Tait either answered or proved did not necessarily support the interpretation Stephenson gave to them. Rather than attempt to add to the discussion of pipe roll interpretation, it is proposed here to take a different approach based upon the comparison of entries in the chancery rolls with those in the pipe rolls. Publication of some of the pipe rolls for the thir-

---

37. Tait, *Medieval English Borough,* pp. 185-193. The Liverpool record cited by Tait from a secondary work is found in *Placita de Quo Warranto,* p. 381b.

teenth century since the studies of Stephenson and Tait makes such comparison feasible for a period of a few years.

In dealing with expenses of carrying out administrative duties imposed by the crown, the burgesses regularly claimed allowances when they accounted for the *firma burgi* at the exchequer. Because the allowances were approved, the claims to expenses must refer to expenses incurred by the burgesses themselves or their officials; the barons of the exchequer would certainly have quashed any attempt to pad the allowances by claims not completely justified. This practice of accounting suggests a method for testing whether the chancery writs addressed to bailiffs implied borough responsibility or were being sent to royal officials upon whom the sole responsibility lay. If expenses for carrying out an order addressed to the bailiffs only were allowed on a pipe roll account rendered by the burgesses, the bailiffs must have been acting as agents of the borough; the responsibility for carrying out the order must have belonged to the community, not to the bailiff as an individual.

In cases where the burgesses' right to elect their own officials is included in their charters, the allowances for expenses incurred in carrying out orders addressed to these officials are found in the pipe roll account of the borough as expected. For example, Northampton obtained the right to elect its own reeves in 1189 with a confirmation in 1200, and the expenses of carrying out royal orders addressed to the reeves are duly allowed in the pipe roll accounts rendered by the "burgesses of Northampton" in 1205 and 1208.[38] Several records of 1242 from Gloucester, where the right of election was obtained in 1200, provide the same assurance for orders addressed to the "bailiffs of Gloucester."[39] On the other hand,

38. *Rot. Litt. Cl.*, I, 30a, 112b; cf. *P.R. 7 John*, p. 256 and *P.R. 10 John*, p. 173.
39. *C.R. 1237-42*, p. 395 and *C.L.R.*, II, 126, 134; cf. Cannon, *P.R. 26 Hen. III*, p. 252.

where the burgesses did not have the *firma burgi* or explicit provision for the election of officials, allowances for orders directed to bailiffs appear elsewhere on the pipe rolls. In 1205 Robert de Roppesleis, who rendered account for the farm of Bristol and is identified elsewhere as the constable of Bristol Castle, claimed allowances from the Bristol account both for orders addressed by the king to "his bailiffs of Bristol" and to himself as constable of Bristol.[40] Similarly at Exeter in 1205 an order to the "mayor and reeve of Exeter" resulted in an allowance on the sheriff's account for Devonshire in the pipe rolls.[41]

The problem is to find both chancery and pipe roll evidence for boroughs which had charters without the explicit right to elect their own officials, but which did have the *firma burgi*. The evidence is limited by the fact that the published pipe rolls available for checking orders in the chancery enrolments cover only the years up to 1212 and the separate rolls for 1230 and 1242. Of the chancery records, the *liberate* rolls begin in 1201 and the close rolls in 1204, but the close rolls for 1208 to 1212 are missing. There are no entries with a definite promise of allowance on the corresponding patent rolls to permit checking with the pipe rolls. Even within these limits, the brevity of the pipe roll accounts sometimes prevents comparison, as at Hertford in 1242 when the entire account reads "Burgenses Hertford' xj l. de firma ville sue de pluribus annis" and may or may not conceal allowances for an entry on the *liberate* roll.[42] No more informative is the entry for Winchester that year which reads "Cives Winton' quater xx l. numero de firma ville sue hoc anno sicut continetur in rotulo xxiiij," or the entries for three years when the city was in

40. *Rot. Litt. Cl.*, I, 6b, 24a, 49b, 50a; cf. *P.R. 7 John*, p. 101.
41. *Rot. Litt. Cl.*, I, 39b; cf. *P.R. 7 John*, p. 19.
42. *C.L.R.*, II, 115; cf. Cannon, *P.R. 26 Hen. III*, p. 217.

the hands of a custodian, but other records are available for this city.[43]

An order by the king to "his bailiffs" of Winchester to purchase a saddle in 1207 is inconclusive because the sheriff was farming the city as *custos* that year.[44] However, the following year the pipe roll account is rendered by the "citizens of Winchester" and the entry includes allowances that correspond to chancery orders addressed "to the reeves" (*prepositis*) on January 30, "to his bailiffs" (*ballivis suis*) on February 3, and the "reeves" on February 4. There is no allowance anywhere on the pipe roll resulting from an order addressed to the "mayor of Winchester" on February 26, but chancery orders frequently did not result in allowances; whether because the orders were not carried out or payment was made by other means is not apparent.[45] On October 4, 1229, a general order to assist William Talebot, who was sent to obtain provisions for the king's crossing to the continent, was addressed as follows: "Rex baillivis Portesmue et omnibus baillivis et fidelibus suis de partibus Suhamtonie, Wintonie et Portesmue, salutem." Although nothing was allowed on the Portsmouth or Southampton accounts, the citizens of Winchester did deduct thirty shillings five pence for this reason.[46] An order to buy lead and take it to Portsmouth for the king's use addressed to the mayor and bailiffs in 1230 is allowed on the account rendered by the citizens.[47] A similar order to the bailiffs of Southampton allowed on the account of the "*Homines*" of Southampton is only one of many orders allowed that year for Southampton.[48]

In fact, the total evidence for Southampton is the fullest for any borough, and with one exception agrees with that of

43. *C.L.R.* II, 129; cf. Cannon, *P.R. 26 Hen. III*, p. 275; *P.R. 6 John*, p. 130.
44. *Rot. Litt. Cl.*, I, 89a; cf. *P.R. 9 John*, pp. 139, 143.
45. *Rot. Litt. Cl.*, I, 101b (twice), 102a, 104a; cf. *P.R. 10 John*, p. 126.
46. *C. R. 1227-31*, p. 270; cf. *P.R. 14 Hen. III*, p. 201.
47. *C.L.R.*, I, 176; cf. *P.R. 14 Hen. III*, p. 200.
48. *C.L.R.*, I, 151; cf. *P.R. 14 Hen. III*, p. 202.

Winchester. Allowances are made for orders addressed to the "bailiffs of Southampton," "reeves of Southampton," "bailiffs of the port of Southampton," "his bailiffs of Southampton," and "bailiffs of the king of Southampton."[49] Because the burgesses of Southampton for some time held the farm of Portsmouth, too, orders to the "bailiffs of Portsmouth" and "bailiffs of the port of Portsmouth" were also allowed in the combined account rendered by Southampton.[50] The exceptional case occurred in 1205 when the bailiffs of Southampton were ordered to provide passage to William Drom, who was being sent as a royal messenger to Normandy, and the cost of his passage was allowed on the account of the sheriff of Sussex.[51] Since the allowance is not made from the same county in which Southampton lay, the most natural explanation is that Drom found it more convenient to take passage elsewhere, but no other order establishing an allowance is enrolled that year. The example of Bristol also agrees with the Winchester evidence and that of Southampton; in 1242 orders to the bailiffs of Bristol are followed by allowances to the citizens on the pipe roll.[52]

These examples establish that the bailiffs in each case were acting in the name of the burgesses, in spite of the fact that there are no known grants of the right to elect their own officials. Although this evidence does not prove that the bailiffs were elected, such election would be the most likely explana-

49. *Rot. Litt. Cl.*, I, 39b, 78b, 89a and *C.R. 1227-31*, p. 339; cf. *P.R. 7 John*, p. 131; *P.R. 9 John*, p. 144; and *P.R. 14 Hen. III*, p. 202 for an example of each type.
50. *Rot. Litt. Cl.*, I, 27b, 81b, 83a and *C.R. 1237-42*, p. 371; cf. *P.R. 7 John*, p. 131; *P.R. 9 John*, pp. 144-145; and Cannon, *P.R. 26 Hen. III*, p. 275.
51. *Rot. Litt. Cl.*, I, 22b; cf. *P.R. 7 John*, pp. 106, 131.
52. *C.L.R.*, II, 78, 115, 130, 139; cf. Cannon, *P.R. 26 Hen. III*, pp. 256-257. Mr. Bryan Little in *The City and County of Bristol* (London, 1954), p. 38 states that it "appears" Henry III gave Bristol license to do as London and elect a mayor and two *prepositores* in place of the sheriff and bailiff in 1216, but he gives no indication of his source. Such a provision is not included in the charters analyzed in *B.B.C.*

tion and would agree with the conclusions of Ballard and Tait that the grant of the *firma burgi* implied the right to elect officials. There can be little doubt that where the burgesses farmed their own revenues any chancery orders sent to the bailiffs meant responsibility for the burgesses as such, not simply the individuals in that office. Therefore, in the succeeding chapter such letters addressed to the officials of any borough which had obtained the *firma burgi* will be considered as evidence of burgess responsibility, and other letters where the burgesses are not included in the salutation and the borough did not have this right or the right of election will be excluded as not conclusively demonstrating responsibility by the burgesses themselves.[53]

Other references show the close connection of the office of bailiff with the collection of revenue and the dual character imposed by responsibility to the borough and to the king. The Assize of Northampton in 1176 provided that "Bailiffs of the lord king should respond at the exchequer both for fixed revenue and for all their profits which they make in their bailiwick, except for those which pertain to the sheriff."[54] In some memoranda rolls of Henry III's reign the sheriffs are ordered to distrain the bailiffs and six men from Stamford and Grimsby in each case to respond for their farm. At York a similar distraint was ordered on behalf of the bailiffs and the city for a debt owed by an individual.[55] At Norwich in 1230 the sheriff was ordered to distrain the bailiffs, reeves, and twelve of the better men to respond for debt for having their liberties, and the bailiffs and six men to respond for tallage and confirmation by the king.[56] The responsibility of a bailiff

53. For grants of *firma burgi,* refer to the Appendix.
54. Paragraph 10. See William Stubbs, ed., *Select Charters and Other Illustrations of English Constitutional History* (9th ed.; Oxford, 1913), p. 181.
55. Memoranda Rolls 28, 52, and 53 Hen. III quoted in Madox, *Firma Burgi,* p. 159 n.
56. *Memoranda Roll 1230-1231,* pp. 26-27.

in carrying out the tasks assigned him by the king as illustrated
by the previous examples was generalized by the lawyers under
Edward I, who held it a principle of law that if a bailiff of a
liberty of the king (such as the city of Hereford) did not obey
the mandate of the king, he should be imprisoned until he paid
his fine to the king.[57]

King Henry III granted the citizens of London their request
of 1266-67 to elect two bailiffs to have custody of London and
Middlesex, and the barons of the exchequer were ordered to
receive them as was customary to respond for the farm. The
bailiffs took an oath to conduct themselves faithfully in that
custody toward the king and the city.[58] Even though the
citizens of Canterbury had obtained the right to elect their
own bailiffs in 1234, an inquest jury in 1275-76 stated that
"the bailiffs of the lord king hold the town of Canterbury of
the lord king in fee farm."[59] In discussing the significance
of the office of mayor as a new step toward the idea of the
city as a legal corporation, J. W. F. Hill makes some helpful
comments on the nature of the office of bailiff:

There was emerging a new aspect of city life. Bailiffs chosen by
the citizens, or at least from among the citizens, there had been
since the early days of Henry II: but the bailiffs were royal officers,
collecting the royal revenues, even though by royal grace the revenues were farmed. The bailiffs' collection belonged to the king,
though when the citizens had the farm of the city there might be

57. *Year Books of the Reign of King Edward the First*, ed. Alfred J. Horwood
(Rolls Series, London, 1866-79), vol. of 20-21 Edward I, 149 (1292).

58. Thomas Madox, *The History and Antiquities of the Exchequer* (London,
1769), II, 96 n. (from Memoranda Roll 51 Hen. III): "Baronibus, pro Civibus Londoniae; Cum Rex, precibus Civium suorum Londoniae annuere volens, concesserit
eisdem Civibus, quod duos Ballivos de se ipsis, Regi & eidem Civitati fideles, eligere
possint ad custodiam Civitatis praedictae & Comitatus Middlesexae, donec Rex de
Consilio suo aliud inde providerit . . . . Ita tamen quod de firma eorundem Regi
respondeant ad Scaccarium, sicut fieri consuevit . . . . et sacramentum praestiterunt,
quod fideliter se habebunt in Custodia praedicta erga Dominum Regem & Civitatem
praedictam, sicut praedictum est."

59. *Rotuli Hundredorum*, I, 55; *B.B.C.*, II, 352.

60. *Medieval Lincoln* (Cambridge, 1948), p. 194.

a surplus which belonged to the citizens collectively, forming the nucleus of a common purse or a common chest. . . .

These comments serve to illustrate the duality of the office of bailiff, although Hill may have stressed the royal aspect of that office unduly to make clear his contrast with that of mayor. A similar idea is involved when the borough of Winchelsea was given to the barons and bailiffs in 1278 to be kept by the bailiffs, so that the barons by the hand of the bailiffs might render forty-two pounds annually and so that each man of the town might contribute according to his means and the poor not be vexed.[61]

The king did not hesitate to use bailiffs of the boroughs as his agents: one of the bailiffs at Lincoln in 1275-76 served as keeper of the works and quarries, the bailiff of Scarborough took land into the king's hand as an escheat in 1303, and the bailiffs of Dunwich assessed the king's right of wreck in 1286 as part of their farm.[62] On another occasion when the bailiffs of Dunwich imprisoned royal messengers who carried writs from the sheriff to be executed in Dunwich because the bailiffs had refused to act, the king took the liberties of Dunwich into his hand.[63] This use of bailiffs by the king provoked an interesting comment on the royal authority by the author of the *Dialogue of the Exchequer*. He is discussing the appointment of men as sheriffs or bailiffs:

Master. It is the King's prerogative as chief of the executive that any man in the kingdom, if the King need him, may be freely taken and assigned to the King's service, whose man soever he be, and whomsoever he serves in war or in peace. Scholar. I see the poet's words are true: "Have you forgotten that kings' arms are long?"[64]

61. *Calendar of the Fine Rolls* (London, 1911), I, 92.
62. *Rotuli Hundredorum*, I, 399; *Calendar of Inquisitions Miscellaneous (Chancery)* (London, 1916) I, 520; *Placita de Quo Warranto*, p. 735a.
63. Sayles, *Select Cases . . . King's Bench*, II, 143-145.
64. Richard Fitz-Nigel, *Dialogus de Scaccario*, translated by Charles Johnson as

In practice, it is clear that all bailiffs, whether appointed by the king or elected, were expected to serve the king in whatever duties were assigned by such letters as those of safe conduct or regulation of commerce addressed "Rex omnibus ballivis portuum maris Anglie. . . ."

Most of the royal letters cited in the following chapters illustrate the activity of bailiffs acting for the burgesses as the chief executive officials of the boroughs. These include letters addressed to the "mayor and bailiffs," "bailiffs and proved men," "barons and bailiffs" in one of the Cinque Ports, and simply "bailiffs" where the burgesses had the right of election or burgess responsibility can be assumed following a grant of *firma burgi*. The bailiff remained throughout the thirteenth century the chief personal contact between the central administration and the boroughs scattered throughout England, an official responsible to the king both for himself and for the burgesses in whose name he acted.

The Course of the Exchequer (N. Y., 1950), p. 84. This edition includes a parallel Latin text established by Arthur Hughes, C. G. Crump, and C. Johnson in their Oxford edition, 1902.

CHAPTER III. FINANCIAL RESPONSI-
BILITIES OF THE BOROUGH

THE use of the borough in local administration, adopted
by royal officials as a practical matter without plan or
pattern of development, expanded during the twelfth century
as a matter partly of convenience and partly of necessity oc-
casioned when a borough gained exemption from the jurisdiction of the sheriff. Because there was no system, it is often
difficult to grasp the bewildering variety of administrative
tasks assumed by the boroughs, and some classification must be
introduced for the sake of clarity, even though there is no
contemporary precedent to place such a classification upon
sound historical footing. It seems best, therefore, to employ
categories that satisfy our ideas of administration, but which
might have surprised the reeves and bailiffs of the twelfth
and thirteenth centuries. First of all, financial responsibilities
should be considered, both because they are among the most
important administrative responsibilities of the boroughs and
because some understanding of finance is necessary in evaluat-
ing the evidence from the pipe rolls, the most important source
from the twelfth century. Later chapters will deal with the

administration of justice, military and naval responsibilities, the regulation of commerce, and miscellaneous responsibilities that fit none of these categories.

The growing use of borough officials by the king seems to parallel the restless activity of Henry II, his sons, and their ministers in developing and perfecting the major organs of the central government, and it is probable that the expansion in use of the boroughs is partly a response to the expansion of the activities of the various departments as they impinged upon local units of government. However, this relationship is to some extent illusory, because allowance must be made for the fact that most of the evidence for the administrative use of boroughs comes from the records of the newly developing departments of the central government and, in consequence, this evidence naturally becomes fuller for the years after additional series of rolls began to be kept by the chancery. The pipe rolls, earliest among the royal records, have been published in series only through the year 1212, but the few printed rolls of the thirteenth century do give some further evidence and, more importantly, provide assurance that the information deduced from pipe rolls does not differ in kind from the information in the chancery rolls of that period.

Drawn up to satisfy the need of the exchequer for a record of royal revenues due and collected, the pipe rolls provide only indirect evidence of the administrative activities of the burgesses and their officials. The first problem in using this evidence is to identify the accountant responsible for the items listed in the borough entry. In those cases where the account is rendered by the sheriff, the administrative activities implied by the statement of allowances made from the farm for expenses in carrying out royal orders probably were performed by the sheriff acting in his capacity as a royal official and charged against the borough farm merely for convenience in accounting. For example, when an allowance for transporting the king's treasure is listed in such an account, there is nothing to indicate that this allowance differs from a similar one in a county account, or that the burgesses or their officials performed any function in relation to the transfer. Possibly the sheriff had made some secondary arrangement whereby the burgesses did the work, but the brief entries on the pipe rolls contain no hint that such arrangements were ever made, thus practically ruling out such an assumption.[1] This argument applies with equal force to an entry where an individual who farmed the revenues of the borough or a royal official acting as *custos* rendered the account.[2] The conclusion must be that only those entries where the burgesses or their officials rendered the account can provide conclusive evidence for administrative responsibilities of the boroughs. Because such entries are found only for those places that had obtained the privilege of the *firma burgi,* this procedure imposes an initial limitation upon the number of boroughs from which evidence of administrative responsibilities is available on the pipe rolls.

The earliest known grant of *firma burgi* in any borough was that made by Henry I to the citizens of Lincoln. In the pipe roll for 1130, the only roll extant from his reign, there is an entry that records a payment from the citizens to the king for the privilege of holding their city from the king "in chief."[3] Although the wording of the entry differs from the better-known grants of *firma burgi* by Henry II, the citizens

1. What lies behind the following entry concerning a borough aid is a matter for conjecture: "Et in perdona per breve Regis Burgensibus de Oxeneforda x li.," *P.R. 31 Hen. I,* p. 6. Possibly some administrative action had been performed, but a more likely explanation is a plea of hardship and inability to pay.

2. The appointment of a royal *custos* involved a shift of responsibility illustrated by the following entry: "Homines de Colecestria Vic. pro eis (ut custos r.c. de). . ." in *P.R. 14 John,* p. 54 (1212). The words in parenthesis are interlined in the original. A similar entry occurs on p. 94 of this roll: "Cives Winton' (Vic. pro eis) r.c. . . . de remanenti firme de anno preterito."

3. *P.R. 31 Hen. I,* p. 114: "Nova Placita et Nove Conventiones. . . . Burgenses Lincolnie reddunt Compotum de cc m. argenti et iij m. auri ut teneantur Ciuitatem de Rege in capite."

seem to have successfully maintained their privilege even during the period of disorder that followed Henry I's death,
for an account made by the reeves of Lincoln in 1155 included
the last few weeks of Stephen's reign.[4] A second grant of *firma
burgi* was included in Henry II's charter to Lincoln (1155-58),
but in this charter there is no mention that the grant was in fee
farm according to the usual wording for later twelfth-century
grants of perpetual *firma burgi*.[5] Apparently, Henry II's grant
was revocable at the king's pleasure, for the farm of Lincoln
was returned to the sheriff in 1157.[6] Render of the account by
the sheriff was only temporary; the reeves of Lincoln rendered
the account in 1164 and continued to do so throughout the rest
of the reign.[7] Richard I brought an interruption in the long
period of burgess farming at Lincoln when he placed the farm
in the hands of the sheriff for 1190, but in 1194 he granted the
farm to the citizens and their heirs from himself and his
heirs, and this grant of fee farm was confirmed in 1200 by
his successor.[8]

The history of burgess farming in London is in direct
contrast to the long and successful tenure of this privilege
by the citizens of Lincoln. Henry I granted the farm of London
and Middlesex to the citizens of London by his charter of
1131,[9] but the Londoners soon lost their privilege after his
death. Both Stephen and Matilda in their rival bids for power
found it expedient to grant the farm of London to Geoffrey de
Mandeville, who thus resumed the position as sheriff that his
father and grandfather had occupied before Henry I's charter.[10]

4. Tait, *Medieval English Borough*, p. 157.
5. *B.B.C.*, I, 221: "Sciatis me liberasse civitatem meam Lincolniam civibus meis
ejusdem civitatis ad illam firmam ad quam solebat esse tempore regis Henrici avi
mei cum omnibus consuetudinibus et libertatibus eidem civitati pertinentibus in
civitatem et extra."
6. *P.R. 4 Hen. II*, p. 136; Tait, p. 162.
7. *P.R. 10 Hen. II*, p. 23; Tait, p. 163.
8. *P.R. 2 Ric. I*, p. 76; Tait, p. 180; *B.B.C.*, I, 221.
9. *B.B.C.*, I, 220.
10. Tait, p. 157.

Although the Londoners obtained a charter from Henry II, that charter did not contain the *firma burgi* clause, and it was not until the pipe roll account for Michaelmas 1191 that they again accounted for their borough farm.[11] The London farm reverted to the sheriffs for two years until Richard I's charter in April 1194.[12] The *firma burgi* clause of that charter was then continued in John's charter of 1199, which provided that the Londoners and their heirs should hold the farm from John and his heirs forever.[13]

Henry II made a number of other grants of *firma burgi* during his reign, but all these grants were revocable at the king's pleasure, and several of the boroughs were not able to retain the privilege after receiving it. The burgesses of Wallingford obtained the *firma burgi* in 1155 and continued to account for their farm for nearly thirty years. Their later accounts show large arrears until 1183, when the final account closed with a large debt of over fifty pounds. For the rest of Henry II's reign, the keeper of the honor of Wallingford also accounted for the borough farm.[14] The burgesses of Grimsby rendered the account for their borough only for the brief period of three months in 1160-61. The following year the sheriff again rendered the account and continued to do so until the fee farm was granted to Grimsby by Henry III in 1227.[15] For a single decade from 1165 to 1176, the burgesses of Gloucester held their borough farm.[16] Although the burgesses of Shrewsbury and Bridgnorth paid to have their borough farm in 1170, they continued to account for their farm to the sheriff for six years before obtaining the right to account directly to the exchequer in return for a further payment.[17]

11. *Ibid.*, p. 163; P.R. *3 Ric. I*, p. 135.
12. P.R. *7 Ric. I*, p. 113; Tait, p. 182.   13. B.B.C., I, 220.
14. P.R. *3 Hen. II*, p. 83; P.R. *29 Hen. II*, p. 70; P.R. *30 Hen. II*, pp. 57-58.
15. P.R. *7 Hen. II*, p. 17; B.B.C., II, 305.
16. P.R. *11 Hen. II*, p. 14; P.R. *23 Hen. II*, p. 42.
17. P.R. *16 Hen. II*, p. 133; P.R. *21 Hen. II*, p. 38; Tait, pp. 174-175.

Northampton and Cambridge in 1184-85 were the last two boroughs to obtain the grant of *firma burgi* from Henry II.[18]

The situation at Southampton during the reign of Henry II was complicated, with the reeves rendering the account from 1165 to 1179, the wife of one of the former reeves appearing for the account at the exchequer until 1182, and accountants identified as borough reeves again rendering the account from 1182 to 1189.[19] By their own statement, the reeves were not farming the borough in 1165 even though they accounted for it at the exchequer, and Tait suggested that they were acting as *custodes* for the king.[20] A more permanent arrangement must have been made during the next year or two, for the statement that the reeves do not hold the borough in farm appears on only one succeeding pipe roll, yet the reeves continued to account for Southampton at the exchequer. In spite of these complications, the accounts of that borough during the years when the reeves rendered them have been used for this study, on the grounds that the authority of the reeves to account for Southampton depended upon their status as borough officials. On the other hand, accounts rendered by the wife of a former reeve have not been used because she seems to have held no official position in the borough except as her husband's heir, although she had served as his deputy before his death. In any case, she was replaced after two years by a new reeve, who

18. *P.R. 31 Hen. II*, p. 46.   For a discussion of grants of *firma burgi* by Henry II, see Tait, pp. 172-176.

19. *P.R. 11 Hen. II*, p. 44: "Rogerus filius Milonis et Fortinus et Robertus de Sancto Laur' reddunt Compotum de firma de Hantona"; *P.R. 13 Hen. II*, p. 194 identifies these men as the "supra dicti prepositi"; *P.R. 25 Hen. II*, pp. 107-108: "Robertus de Sancto Laurentio uxor ejus pro eo redd, comp. de cc li. blancorum de firma de Hanton' . . . . Cecilia uxor Roberti de Sancto Laurentio redd. Comp. de c m. de promissione sua pro debitis viri sui habendis, et ballia de Hanton' tenenda usque ad festum Sancti Michaelis"; *P.R. 28 Hen. II*, p. 147: "Geruasius de Hantona"; *P.R. 31 Hen. II*, p. 214 identifies Geruasius as "prepositus de Sudhantona."

20. *P.R. 12 Hen. II*, p. 109: (account of three reeves) "Sed dicunt quod non habent uillam de Hantona ad firmam"; *P.R. 13 Hen. II*, p. 194 (same reeves' account) "Sed clamant Regis warantum quod non tenuerunt uillam ad firmam"; see the discussion in Tait, p. 170.

continued to account for Southampton during the remainder of Henry II's reign.

The policy of Richard and John was to grant charters and the *firma burgi* privilege liberally to those burgesses willing to pay for such concessions. Richard I's urgent need for money caused him to grant or confirm this privilege for seven boroughs during the first few weeks of his reign. Of more importance for municipal development, he introduced a basic change from his father's policy when he began to grant the *firma burgi* to a number of boroughs in perpetuity. During the reigns of Richard and John, the new grants of perpetual farm far outnumbered those made according to the old policy with grants revocable at the king's pleasure.[21] As a practical advantage for this study, the rapid expansion of these grants of *firma burgi* provides an increasing number of accounts in the pipe rolls that contain clear evidence of the administrative functions performed by the boroughs. In using the pipe rolls, the principle has been followed that no account for a borough should be used unless it is clear that the burgesses, either directly or through their officials, were responsible for making the account in which allowances were claimed.

This practice of making allowances at the exchequer for expenses incurred in performance of duties for the king had already been firmly established in sheriffs' accounts at the time of the first extant pipe roll for 1130, and the practice continued without interruption after the burgesses had obtained the *firma burgi,* as shown by statements of allowances credited in the earliest borough accounts. Indeed the form in the pipe roll accounts ordinarily follows much the same general pattern used by exchequer scribes for the sheriff's statement of his return for the county: name of the accountant,

21. Tait, pp. 178-179. For the dates of grants of *firma burgi,* see the chart in the Appendix.

deduction of fixed payments, deduction of other allowances against the farm, and a statement of revenue collected outside the farm. Except for this general order of entries, there is a noticeable lack of uniformity in accounts for boroughs, even in the position of the accounts on the pipe rolls. The London and Middlesex accounts are the most uniform of all throughout the pipe rolls because they are always set off by large headings in the same manner as county returns and are long enough to contain several well-defined sections. The accounts of a few boroughs, such as Lincoln and Southampton, frequently were placed in a semi-independent position at the end of the account for the county in which these boroughs were located.[22] Sometimes borough accounts were placed on the pipe rolls completely separate from their county, but such a method of entering borough accounts does not seem to have implied any special degree of autonomy in the borough and, more often than not, was simply the result of a clerical error or lack of space on the membrane where the borough account would ordinarily appear.[23] A final method of entering borough accounts was simply to allot a few lines to the borough within the sheriff's account of the county. The best examples are the accounts from Shrewsbury and Bridgnorth, which were placed consistently in the same position on the sheriff's return for the county year after year, even after both boroughs had obtained the *firma burgi* in 1175-76.[24]

A more significant difference among the accounts is that some are much more informative than others because of the amount of detailed information included; conversely, some accounts are of very little value for the study of the administrative

22. For example, *P.R. 11 Hen. II*, p. 39; *P.R. 14 Hen. II*, p. 189.
23. *P.R. 6 Hen. II*, p. 39 (Carlisle).
24. *P.R. 16 Hen. II*, p. 133, and succeeding rolls. The position of these accounts remains the same in the latest roll published: Henry L. Cannon, ed., *The Great Roll of the Pipe for the Twenty-Sixth Year of the Reign of King Henry the Third A.D. 1241-42* (New Haven and London, 1918), p. 1.

responsibilities of the borough because they contain only a brief statement of the amount of the borough farm for the year and its payment into the treasury. It is well to keep these characteristics of a pipe roll in mind because most of the administrative functions of the borough appear only as the result of an allowance approved by the barons of the exchequer, although some other responsibilities can be deduced from judicial fines assessed when burgesses failed to fulfil these responsibilities.[25] In the absence of records like the chancery rolls until the thirteenth century, we cannot be sure that all the administrative tasks of a borough are included, for those tasks performed by the borough without compensation from the king would not appear in any records unless they were fixed by terms of the charter.

With the early years of the thirteenth century the chancery enrolments serve to clarify the (all too often) cryptic references in the pipe rolls and supplement the information found there. Letters close and patent contain direct orders from the king to the officials of the borough, or to the officials and the burgesses. Here we are seeing the first step in the administrative process, with orders that often resulted later in allowances listed on the pipe roll account as the final step in the process. In most respects these direct orders are much more satisfying than inferences made from allowances on a pipe roll. Yet the account on the pipe roll does have the advantage of proving that the royal order had been executed before an allowance was claimed, whereas two or three successive letters close carrying the same royal order serve as a reminder that burgesses did

---

25. For an example of a dispute over allowances at the exchequer accounting, see *Memoranda Roll 1230-1231,* p. 17: "Homines de Colcest' habent diem super compotum vicecomitis proximum ad ostendendum cartam suam . ut per illam videatur quomodo tenent uillam suam . et a quo tempore . et utrum iiij^{or} li. in defalta monetariorum et xl s. in bosco de Colcestr' debeat [*sic,* ed.] eis allocari vel non." Certainly making allowances for default of moneyers was no novelty. In 1211 the burgesses of Colchester were credited with 4 li. and the burgesses at Norwich and Ipswich each with 6 li. for this reason. *P.R. 13 John,* pp. 15, 119.

not always act just as commanded by a royal writ. In regard to the financial responsibilities of the borough, the records of both the exchequer and the chancery are particularly valuable in supplementing each other to provide the full picture.

The privilege of the *firma burgi* has been discussed in reference to its importance for the interpretation of evidence from the pipe rolls, but some emphasis should also be given to the fact that the collection of the borough farm was in itself an important administrative responsibility for the burgesses. The success of transferring this responsibility from the sheriff to the burgesses provided a precedent for later transfer of other responsibilities, and provided the administrative experience necessary for the borough officials to undertake them. However, the burgesses could call upon the support of royal authority in cases of difficulty in collecting the revenues that made up the farm either by pleadings at the exchequer or in another royal court. Disagreement over the right of the burgesses of Huntingdon to collect farm from some lands of the abbot and monks of Thorney resulted in a compromise duly recorded at the exchequer in 1219.[26] One way in which royal authority might be asserted in support of burgesses was illustrated when the citizens of Norwich attempted to excuse themselves in 1237 for arrears in their farm and tallage on the grounds that the tenants of the Prior of Norwich within the city would not join them in paying. The Prior attempted to argue against the citizens, but the barons of the exchequer informed him that it was the king who summoned him to answer, not the citizens. The barons concluded the case with the observation that it seemed to them that all who have a part in the liberties and merchant rights of a city ought to pay toward the farm.[27] The same

26. Hilary Jenkinson and E. R. F. Beryl, eds., *Select Cases in the Exchequer of Pleas* (Selden Society, 48, London, 1932), p. xxxv (from Memoranda Roll for 1219).

27. *Ibid.*, pp. 16-19.

rule had been laid down in the *curia regis* in reference to Worcester with this statement: "if the men of this town do not have the farm owed to the lord king, all of this town, whosoever men they may be . . . shall aid in raising the farm. . . ."[28] On the other hand, failure to prove a claim that certain men ought to aid in paying the borough farm brought a fine against the burgesses of Bedford for a false claim.[29]

From the collection of royal revenues that made up the farm for the borough to the collection of other special assessments was an easy transition both for the ministers of the king and for the burgesses. To the royal government such a method offered a way of collecting money with the least resentment and without adding to the burden of the sheriff or creating special collectors; the burgesses had already found out that their interests were furthered by assessing themselves rather than having sheriffs or other royal officials operating freely within the borough to collect money. In this connection, an examination of the pipe rolls shows that the borough served as an important source of revenue beyond the income from the farm, a source frequently exploited by the kings from the time of Henry II by means of a succession of aids, gifts, assizes, or tallages. Of course, the administrative significance of this taxation upon the boroughs lies in the method of assessment and collection adopted, for the burgesses themselves often made agreements with the royal officials to produce certain sums from the borough and undertook the details of collecting these sums themselves.

The development of a royal tax on the borough can be traced in the pipe rolls from the early experimental stage until the regularization of the tallage in the later years of Henry II's reign. The pipe roll of 1130 shows that for at least three

28. *Curia Regis Rolls*, IX, 353 (1220).
29. *Ibid.*, XI, 178 (1223).

years previously round sums called *auxilia* had been assessed along with the customary Danegeld. Although Henry II continued this assessment introduced by his grandfather by collecting aids from the boroughs in connection with Danegelds in the second and eighth years of his reign, the pipe rolls make it clear that a new tax was being developed; this was later regularized under the name of tallage. When Henry II took his last Danegeld with *auxilia* from the boroughs in 1162, the period of experimentation was over and the *dona* and other assessments made under various names had been developed into a tax identical with the later tallage in everything but name. During the remaining years of his reign, Henry II made only five general levies—in 1165, 1168-69, 1173-74, 1177, and 1187. The important characteristic of these levies as they applied to the borough was that they were separately negotiated roughly on the basis of cash resources in each borough rather than being fixed amounts.[30]

The primary impression gained from an examination of tallage in the pipe rolls of Richard I is that the various tallages during this reign were very unevenly distributed among the counties. The first tallage of the reign was assessed in 1194 but was reported by only eight counties on the pipe roll for 1195. Some counties reported this tallage on the following pipe roll, but other counties were reporting a new tallage assessed in 1195. Two counties listed a tallage assessed in 1196, but very little additional evidence can be found in any of the pipe rolls for a tallage in that year. The last tallage of Richard's reign was taken in 1197-98 in connection with scutage from the royal tenants-in-chief.[31]

Tallages continued to be a heavy burden on the boroughs

30. Stephenson, *Borough and Town*, pp. 160-166, 170-171, and Appendix IV, pp. 222-223.
31. Doris M. Stenton, "Introduction" to the following pipe rolls: *P.R. 7 Ric. I*, p. xxiv; *P.R. 8 Ric. I*, pp. xxi-xxii; *P.R. 9 Ric. I*, p. xiii; *P.R. 10 Ric. I*, p. xxiv.

during the reigns of John and Henry III. John took a tallage during the first year of his reign to finance an expedition to Normandy against Philip Augustus, and after a lapse of only about a year, a new tallage appears almost every year for several years. The average frequency of tallage under John and his son, Henry III, was one tallage levied every three years; John levied six or eight tallages in the seventeen years of his reign and Henry took fifteen tallages in fifty-six years.[32] Other taxes were used to supplement these tallages, among them taxes on movables, which came to succeed tallage as the usual form of taxation after 1272.[33]

The active role taken by the burgesses in the negotiation of amounts to be assessed gave them important administrative functions as described by Richard Fitz-Nigel in the *Dialogus de Scaccario* in his explanation of the procedure employed by the justices of Henry II's reign in assessing a *donum vel aux-ilium*. The justices might assess the sum on a per capita basis, or the burgesses might offer a sum acceptable to the justices for the whole borough. In the case of a per capita assessment, the individual burgess was liable to the extent of his property and his rents for failure to pay his assessment, but in the case of composition between the burgesses and the justices, the obligation to pay the agreed sum was shared by all the burgesses. If a borough failed to pay the full amount, the sheriff made an inquiry and pledged those burgesses who were insolvent when the agreement was made. The rest of the burgesses had to find some way to meet the deficiency caused by the default of those who were insolvent. They might assess the wealthier burgesses for the amount of the deficiency, or they might apportion that amount equally among all the solvent burgesses. However, the

32. Sydney K. Mitchell, *Studies in Taxation under John and Henry III* (New Haven and London, 1914), p. 340 *passim*. Mitchell in this book described each tallage in detail.

33. Sydney K. Mitchell, *Taxation in Medieval England* (Yale Historical Publications, Studies, XV, New Haven, 1951), pp. 222, 237.

crown was willing to wait for its money from any burgesses who had become insolvent since the agreement with the justices was made.[34]

This method of assessment for tallage by negotiation between the royal officials and the separate boroughs was used during the reigns of Henry's sons and became the usual method of assessment throughout the thirteenth century.[35] Even so, the instructions given to the assessors of the tallage to prevent unfair taxation of the poor show that some supervision was given borough officials in collecting the tax.[36] Royal courts also aided when residents within some boroughs attempted to claim immunities from payment of tallage, and there is one example of a royal order to the sheriff of Kent to take property from a man who had left Canterbury after the assessment of tallage without paying his share.[37] In 1257 the lesser burgesses in Oxford drew up a long list of charges in which they attempted to show that the mayor and jurats had assessed tallage only on them, while the magnates were not forced to pay anything.[38] A maximum emphasis upon the element of negotiation appears in the offer of the proved men of Dunwich and Yarmouth to furnish ships for the king's crossing to the continent in lieu of tallage, and the subsequent agreement by the king to postpone the tallage on condition that he might either require the burgesses of Dunwich to furnish forty ships and the burgesses of Yarmouth to send the ships offered or later require the tallage if he saw fit to do so.[39] In such negotiations, the boroughs seem to have been protected against arbitrary expan-

34. Fitz-Nigel, *Dialogus de Scaccario* (1950 ed.), pp. 108-109.
35. *P.R. 7 Ric. I*, pp. 182, 211; *P.R. 8 Ric. I*, p. 66; *The Memoranda Roll for the Tenth Year of the Reign of King John (1207-8)*, ed. R. A. Brown (Pipe Roll Soc., n.s. LXIX, London, 1957), p. 29; *Curia Regis Rolls*, I, 418; *Rot. Litt. Cl.*, I, 421a; Mitchell, *Studies in Taxation*, p. 294.
36. Mitchell, *Studies in Taxation*, p. 294.
37. *Select Cases in the Exchequer of Pleas*, pp. 16-18; *C.R. 1227-31*, p. 532; *C.R. 1251-53*, p. 165.
38. *Calendar of Inquisitions Miscellaneous (Chancery)*, I, 79-83.
39. *Rot. Litt. Cl.*, II, 174b.

sion of tallage by an idea in the minds of both the burgesses and royal officials of the legitimate amount fixed by an appeal to *lex et consuetudo*.[40]

London provides the best example of the process of collecting these tallages because the citizens possessed unusual bargaining power in their financial relation to the king, were exceptionally zealous in safeguarding their liberties, and, on occasion, did not hesitate to assert claims to even greater liberties. The mayor and sheriffs, both types of officials elected by the citizens, shared the responsibility for collecting tallage, although they might delegate the task to the aldermen and four to six men in each ward.[41] The details of carrying out this responsibility are seen in a case from the mayor's court in 1299 concerned with a butcher who was charged with resisting the sheriff and town clerk when they attempted to levy his portion of a tallage.[42] Both the importance of the financial resources of London to the king and the zeal of the citizens in upholding their liberties can be inferred from a letter patent issued by Henry III in 1226 in which he acknowledged an aid from the citizens with the statement that they had given this aid to help him recover some of his inheritance on the Continent and that such an extraordinary aid would not be held as a precedent against them or their heirs.[43] Ultimately, the responsibility lay with the citizens themselves who elected the officials, as is shown by a letter close of 1227 in which the king threatened to seize the city and its liberties into his hand for failure to collect a tallage and deliver the money to royal officials, unless compliance came within a month.[44]

The collection of tallage was one of the several points where

40. Mitchell, *Taxation in Medieval England,* p. 342.
41. *Rot. Litt. Cl.,* I, 461a-b; *Pat. R.,* II, 132.
42. A. H. Thomas, *Calendar of Early Mayor's Court Rolls . . . A.D. 1298-1307* (Cambridge, 1924), p. 38.
43. *Pat. R.,* II, 104.
44. *C.R. 1227-31,* p. 383.

the issue often was drawn between royal authority and city liberties of London. Powerful and important to the king as the Londoners were, they could not withstand the king and, in the final analysis, were forced to yield or find themselves answering to the dictates of a royal *custos*. In one such dispute between the citizens and royal authority a memorandum was inserted in the close rolls for 1255 providing a permanent record of an unsuccessful claim by the London citizens that they were not liable for tallage. Although the Londoners offered two thousand marks "in the name of an aid," instead of the three thousand marks sought by royal officials as a tallage, the king ordered his officials either to receive the tallage or to collect that amount themselves by assessing the Londoners on a per capita basis. In a second deliberation, the king ordered his clerks to search the rolls, where precedents were found that proved the city had paid tallage several times in the past, and the mayor and citizens were finally forced to admit that they were tallageable and to pay the three thousand marks.[45]

Royal intervention into city affairs in 1257 came because the king had received an anonymous charge that the mayor of London was oppressive. He ordered a royal official to summon the London folkmoot for the purpose of finding out what rich men had been favored in collecting tallage, what poor men had been oppressed, and whether the mayor and his council had diverted part of the tallage for their own use. The case became more and more complicated as other issues were introduced by the populace, who opposed the ruling group in the city, and, finally, amercements were levied on all the accused officials, but nothing was proved unjust about the tallage assessment.[46] Later royal inquiries at London and Northampton seem to show that city officials and rich citizens had obtained

45. *C.R. 1254-56*, pp. 159-160.
46. *Cronica Maiorum et Vicecomitum Londoninarum*, pp. 30-31, 33.

royal charters with exemptions from tallage and thus had shifted the entire burden upon the less wealthy segment of the population.[47]

The experience of the boroughs in compounding for tallage provided a precedent for the active role taken by the burgesses in the assessment and collection of the taxes on movables during the thirteenth century. The earliest of these taxes on movables, the Saladin tithe of 1188, involved a group of the wealthier men of each borough who were summoned to meet with the king, but the presence of the king in person indicates this was an unusual demand and not a routine assessment, as were the later taxes on movables.[48] The history of this type of taxation includes occasional levies under Richard and John; Henry III's levies of 1225, 1232, 1237, 1269; and the two levies of Edward I in 1275 and 1283.[49] The method of assessment used at the close of Henry III's reign was by special negotiation between the small council and the towns without authorization from the great council. The burgesses gained in this type of assessment by keeping the royal officials out of their boroughs and probably by keeping the rate lower than might have otherwise been imposed. How this process worked is illustrated by letters addressed on August 2, 1301, to mayors, bailiffs, and whole communities of most boroughs informing them that the king had appointed two officials to conduct certain of his affairs which they would explain orally and commanding these borough officials to obey orders delivered in the king's name. In his instructions to the royal officials, the king urged them to add as much as possible to the sums collected from a fifteenth in 1290 and suggested they stress the king's need for

47. *Rotuli Hundredorum*, I, 403; II, 2.
48. Mitchell, *Studies in Taxation*, p. 69.
49. James F. Willard, *Parliamentary Taxes on Personal Property 1290 to 1334* (Cambridge, Mass., 1934), p. 3.

money to carry out his projects in Scotland.[50] This process of special negotiation, temporarily abandoned in 1282, lasted until 1295, when the new policy of summoning representatives of the boroughs to meet in parliament provided another method of binding burgesses to an assessment for taxes that was permanently adopted.[51]

The business of collecting the taxes on movables usually fell to the officials of the borough, both where assessment was made for the tax and where the boroughs offered a lump sum as a fine to avoid the more detailed assessment. As was to be expected, these collections did not always proceed without incident, and some of these incidents throw light upon the work of borough officials in collecting a royal levy. The proved men of Bristol were told to deliver the receipts from a fifteenth to the royal official in charge at Winchester, where they could make an accounting before his court.[52] Unable to pay their assessment for a fifteenth, the burgesses of Nottingham were forced to borrow nineteen pounds from one of their number and resort to forceable seizure of property in cases where a burgess either would not or could not pay his portion of the assessment necessary to repay the loan.[53] Examples of compounding for a fifteenth on movables in 1301 are the fines entered on the patent rolls of 2,500 marks paid by London, 200 pounds by Oxford, 400 pounds by Lincoln, and 200 pounds by Northampton.[54] Three years later a potential taxpayer named John le Letour protested successfully against payment of a fifteenth in London by producing a charter which satisfied the mayor and alderman that he was exempt from such taxes.[55]

50. *C.C.R. 1296-1302*, pp. 461-463. For a fuller discussion of this tax see Willard, pp. 131-132.
51. Mitchell, *Taxation in Medieval England*, pp. 220, 229-233.
52. *Rot. Litt. Cl.*, II, 82a.   53. *Select Cases . . . King's Bench*, III, 46 (1296).
54. *C.P.R. 1292-1301*, pp. 602, 603, 605, 608.
55. Reginald R. Sharpe, ed., *Calendar of Letter-Books . . . of the City of London. Letter-Book C* (London, 1901), p. 138.

In addition to the administrative duties that fell to the burgesses and their officials in collecting taxes, the boroughs were being used in the collection of import duties early in the thirteenth century, long before they were incorporated as an integral part of the true customs system that developed in the last quarter of that century. Since Southampton was particularly outstanding in the wine trade, it provides a good example of the use of borough officials for collecting the royal prize on wine. The bailiffs of Southampton seem to have shared the responsibility with a special official, the king's *custos vinorum,* but the exact jurisdiction of each official and his duties is not clear.[56] A royal letter close notified the mayor and bailiffs of Southampton in 1243 that merchants were landing wines at Hamble to avoid having prize taken, although this was against the liberties of Southampton. The local officials were ordered to take action forcing such ships to enter the port as they should, in order that borough officials could take the royal prize and the customs of their town.[57] The joint responsibility of royal officials and local officials was not unique to Southampton, for a similar sharing took place in both Portsmouth and Bristol.[58]

The officials of many other boroughs also collected the prize on wine at times as part of the ordinary procedure used in collecting this levy.[59] Although the merchants were compensated for wine taken as prize, such seizures developed into a tax during the thirteenth century, for the sum allowed the merchants remained at twenty shillings per tun, while the general price level including the price of wine rose throughout

56. Examples of the sort of indirect references which support this conclusion may be found in *P.R. 10 Ric. I,* p. 23; *P.R. 9 John,* p. 145; *P.R. 14 Hen. III,* p. 202; *Rot. Litt. Cl.,* I, 45b, 116a, 460b, 495a, 604a; II, 25b; *C.R. 1256-59,* p. 8; *C.C.R. 1272-79,* p. 22.

57. *C.R. 1242-47,* p. 135.

58. *C.P.R. 1247-58,* pp. 185, 277; *C.L.R.,* III, 276.

59. *C.R. 1227-31,* p. 286; *C.R. 1231-34,* pp. 86, 105; *Pat. R.,* II, 504; *Calendar of the Fine Rolls,* I, 248, 250; *Rotulorum Originalium Abbreviatio,* I, 57.

the period.[60] Some idea of the amount of wine taken for prize in the various boroughs is given by the records kept by the king's butler for 1290-91 when he accounted for the prize at London, Bristol, Newcastle, Boston, Ipswich, Sandwich, and Yarmouth. The total amount seized was 224 tuns, with compensation computed at twenty shillings except at Bristol where the rate was only fifteen shillings, and the expenses of storage and transportation were charged to the account.[61]

The administrative machinery set up for collecting a fifteenth on French merchandise levied by King John in 1203 depended heavily upon the use of burgesses and deserves some attention as a matter of precedent in the use of burgesses, even though it was an exceptional levy. Three royal officials were named "chief wardens of the fifteenth," and six, seven, or more of the leading men were to be chosen in each port to serve together with one knight and one clerk as "bailiffs of the fifteenth." These local men were given broad powers over commerce. The chancery record is damaged at this point, but the sense of the earlier clauses seems to be that for the duration of the war all French merchants should pay a fifteenth on merchandise brought into England except grain, wine, salt, wax, certain types of cloth, and fodder. English merchants were required to list their merchandise and to submit to some regulation concerning the places where they could trade. Foreign merchants were prohibited from bringing any counterfeit or debased coinage into England, and any such coins brought into a port in spite of this prohibition were to be retained in common custody of the bailiffs of the fifteenth. No merchant should presume to load or unload any merchandise except by view and license of the bailiffs, all letters of safe

60. N. S. B. Gras, *The Early English Customs System* (Cambridge, Mass., 1918), pp. 41-42.
61. *Ibid.*, pp. 200-203.

conduct had to be approved by these same men, and steersmen and sailors were required to swear that they would not load or transport any merchandise except by license of the bailiffs. The bailiffs were to keep the money derived from the fifteenth in their common custody until it could be delivered to the chief wardens. Furthermore, they were required to keep a record of the money received, the names of the merchants from whom each payment was received, the date, and the name of the man who sealed the amount with the seal of the chief wardens. The bailiffs were exempted from appearing in court and from tallage, along with other compensations that can no longer be deciphered in the original roll. The enforcement of the more rigid controls of exports and commerce in the concluding clauses of the assize seems to have been the responsibility of the chief wardens only.[62]

Letters close sent to all the ports in the following year probably refer to continuing enforcement of this same assize, but the original record is defective and some words are apparently missing.[63] The defense made by twelve men from Portsmouth in answer to the charge that they had allowed ships to leave their port without paying the fifteenth was that, of the three ships involved, one, from Exeter, had a writ from the bailiffs of Dartmouth certifying that they had already taken the fifteenth, a second had paid ten marks at Portsmouth, and the third, from Winchelsea, had been released when the

---

62. *Rot. Litt. Pat.*, pp. 42a-43a. For a discussion of this customs regulation, see Gras, pp. 48-50.

63. *Rot. Litt. Cl.*, I, 57a. The responsibility of borough officials to keep some royal assize is quite certain, but whether or not this particular assize is meant is not clear. The pertinent sentence is: "Precipimus vobis [bailiffs of all the ports] quod sicut vos ipsos et vestra diligitis de cetero custodiri faciatis in portu . . . [damaged] . . . assisam . . . [damaged] . . . marina nostra prout dilecti et fideles nostri W. de Wrotham Arch' Tant' et Regin' de Cornhull' [named chief wardens of the fifteenth in *Rot. Litt. Pat.*, p. 42a] . . . constituent. . . ." Furthermore, one clause in the assize of the fifteenth does call upon sheriffs, constables, reeves, and all bailiffs of the seaports to aid the chief wardens in their task. See *Rot. Litt. Pat.*, p. 42b.

master found pledges to insure that the cargo of wine would be kept within the realm.[64]

The development of a true customs system was begun in the last quarter of the thirteenth century when policies concerning the customs differed from preceding attempts because they had greater influence on the later customs system and were of longer duration.[65] Parliament granted the custom of 1275 on wool, woolfells, and hides exported from England and Wales; and the people in each port where the king's writs did not run elected two of their number to serve as collectors. These local men took an oath to collect and receive faithfully the established customs, for which they would respond to the king.[66] Although no original or copy of the grant is extant, a note on a fine roll contains the information that these two locally elected officials were to have custody of one part of a royal seal and that the other part would be in the custody of a royal appointee.[67] In 1282 the king ordered several sheriffs and the constable of Dover to go in person to Yarmouth, Ispwich, Dunwich, Winchelsea, Bristol, and Exeter, where they were to cause two men to be chosen from each to collect the king's new custom on wool, fells, and hides.[68] An order by the king and his council in 1297 closed all ports for the export of wool and hides except Newcastle-on-Tyne, Hull, Boston, Yarmouth, Ipswich, London, Sandwich, Southampton, and Bristol. In each of these ports the guardians of the king's custom were to associate two men with themselves to guard the port and regulate shipping.[69] In 1299 the bailiffs and collectors of customs on wool in ten ports were ordered to make the proclamation that no wool was to be taken out of the realm until the king ordered otherwise.[70] According to a letter close of 1304

64. *Curia Regis Rolls*, III, 96.
66. Stubbs, *Select Charters*, pp. 443-444.
68. *C.C.R. 1279-88*, p. 154.
70. *Ibid.*, p. 266.

65. Gras, p. 59.
67. Printed by Gras, p. 223.
69. *C.C.R. 1296-1304*, pp. 86-87.

addressed to Lyme and Exeter, along with other places not having borough status, the practice of electing two men from the boroughs to collect customs was applied to payments and customs granted the king by foreign merchants.[71] That the customs machinery was used for regulating commerce, as well as for collecting a financial levy, is illustrated when the mayor and bailiffs of Chichester were ordered in 1304 to proclaim and enforce the prohibition that no one was permitted to export wool, woolfells, or hides from Chichester. Furthermore, the king commanded that his seal called the "coket" should no longer be used in that port. Similar letters were sent to Winchelsea and Bristol.[72]

Resistance by the citizens of London to the new duties imposed upon them by the royal customs policy is described in municipal records. A writ dated November 19, 1303, carried the royal command to the mayor and aldermen of London to have two collectors elected for the customs on wool, woolfells, and hides in their city and to present them at the exchequer by the second of February. The London officials answered that because the writ was not delivered until the eve of February 2, there had been no time to execute this order, and that they had arrested the chancery messenger for his negligence in the matter. Probably the true reason for failure to carry out this royal command was given in the answer to a second writ on February 16 when the Londoners asserted that the collectors of the customs of the king in their city had been appointed previously by the king and his council, that the citizens had never appointed such officials, and that, accordingly, nothing had been done to carry out the royal command.[73] Although this incident represents but one of the disputes between the Londoners and royal officials over liberties claimed by the citi-

71. *C.C.R. 1302-07*, p. 204.
72. *Ibid.*, p. 123.
73. Sharpe, *Calendar of Letter-Books. Letter-Book C.*, pp. 132, 135.

zens, it does provide a clear example of resistance on the part of burgesses to the imposition of new administrative duties.

In addition to serving the royal administration in collecting taxes and customs duties, the burgesses were called upon to assume responsibilities in making loans or acting as sureties for loans to the king. King John broached the subject of a loan in a letter sent in 1215 from the Continent to all the boroughs and demesne lands in England by reserving his request for the loan (which he promised to repay fully) until he had explained that his campaign in Picardy was going well and that he had received letters from the pope allowing the relaxation of the Interdict in England.[74] A loan which Henry III asked from the men of Chester and of Shrewsbury in June 1244 to meet the expenses of the Welsh war was carried through the pipe rolls until 1286 before an explanation was finally entered.[75] Henry III was quite direct in 1255 when he ordered borough officials at London and York to pay a bond given by the king to the merchants of Lucca for wares taken from them for use of the king and his son Edward, thus initiating a short-term loan because money for this purpose was to be subtracted from the tallage of those cities.[76] A commentary on the incident was provided the following year when the king instructed the barons of the exchequer not to admit to their offices the men elected as sheriffs and mayor of London when they presented themselves for confirmation until the Londoners paid the king's debts to the merchants of Lucca.[77]

On a less weighty matter, the mayor of Lynn was once ordered to aid the king by paying merchants at the fair of Lynn for goods taken by the king's bailiffs, with the promise that the

74. *Rot. Litt. Pat.*, p. 111b.
75. Mabel Mills and R. Stewart-Brown, eds., *Cheshire in the Pipe Rolls* (The Record Society for the Publication of Original Documents Relating to Lancashire and Cheshire, XCII, n.p., 1938), pp. 83, 85-86.
76. *C.P.R. 1247-58*, p. 404.
77. *C.R. 1254-56*, p. 361.

king would cause him to have the money at London after the close of the fair.[78] More frequently than making loans, the burgesses were asked to stand as sureties for the king, whether to the citizens of Bordeaux and La Rochelle in regard to loans for as much as 1500 marks or on the domestic scene to satisfy winesellers and merchants selling provisions for the king's Christmas feast.[79]

The burgesses' side of the arrangements in making a loan to a king is exposed to view in a detailed entry placed in the municipal records of London in 1299. First, a copy of a letter patent gives the information that the Londoners had undertaken to satisfy Gascon creditors of the king for a debt amounting to more than a thousand pounds; the king had granted the Londoners their farm and other issues usually reported to the exchequer until that sum had been raised in repayment of their loan.[80] Next follows a long list of debts owed by the king's Gascon creditors to men of London or the immediate surrounding area because the mayor and aldermen pursued the indirect, yet cautious and practical, course of making payments to their fellow citizens in cancellation of debts owed by the Gascons in London, rather than by making direct payments to the Gascons for the debts owed them by the king. Two letters patent issued under the seal of the commonalty of London follow in the record for October and November of 1299, and these provide a receipt to the sheriffs for forty pounds which they had delivered to the mayor and aldermen out of the issues of the shrievalty in pursuance of the king's grant. A letter issued by the Londoners on November 20, 1299, records the payment of twenty-eight pounds that they had made for debts owed the Gascons. Finally, another receipt is given for money

78. *Rot. Litt. Cl.*, I, 365b.
79. *Pat. R.*, I, 211, 256, 303-304. For a discussion of these loans, see Kate Norgate, *The Minority of Henry the Third* (London, 1912), p. 176. *C.R. 1256-59*, pp. 269-270; *C.R. 1261-64*, pp. 14-15.
80. Sharpe, *Letter-Book C*, p. 44; see also *C.P.R. 1292-1301*, p. 418.

received from the sheriffs out of the London farm.[81] In a trans-
action two years later the same arrangements for repayment
were made when the Londoners acted as surety for five hundred pounds to merchants who had refused to sell goods directly to the royal wardrobe.[82]

Unlike the various financial responsibilities that have
been discussed, the responsibilities of the burgesses in connection with regulations about coinage and exchanges involved
not only the administration of a predetermined royal policy,
but on occasion also involved giving advice before the formu-
lation of that policy. In regard to these matters the burgesses
were obviously in the position of possessing expert knowledge
qualifying them for more than routine usefulness confined to
matters of administration. The use of burgesses in safeguarding
against clipped or counterfeit coins is found in 1204 when four
men in each borough, castle, or vill where there was a market
were selected to seize and perforate such coins, and in the
following year when the free and law-worthy men in cities,
boroughs, and vills were to serve on juries to inquire about
persons clipping coins.[83] Borough officials took their place
alongside royal officials in both proclaiming and enforcing the
king's regulations in regard to the royal exchanges and coinage.[84] Something more than usual resistance to royal policies
must lie behind an order to the mayor and sheriffs of London
in 1241 to have several goldsmiths come to their court and
take an oath there in the presence of the treasurer and the
warden of the exchange that they would not break the assize
of metals or act against the exchange.[85]

Burgesses participated directly in the organization of royal

81. Sharpe, pp. 45-54.
82. *Ibid.*, p. 90.
83. *Rot. Litt. Pat.*, pp. 47-48, 54b.
84. *Pat. R.*, I, 359; II, 502; *C.R. 1247-51*, p. 9; *C.P.R.* 1247-58, p. 15; *Cronica
Maiorum et Vicecomitum*, p. 13.
85. *C.R. 1237-42*, p. 322.

exchanges in 1247 and 1248. The king ordered borough officials of Norwich and Winchester to elect four faithful men from each of their boroughs to manage the royal exchanges and to provide secure buildings for use as an exchange and in safeguarding the king's money used in the operation.[86] At these cities, plus Exeter, Lincoln, and Northampton, the election of financial officials in 1248 included four moneyers, four wardens of the mint, and two goldsmiths as assayers, whose names were all to be presented for approval at the exchequer according to custom. With the burgesses providing the personnel, the king's brother planned to deliver one thousand pounds sterling to each place to be used for sustaining the exchange and for fabricating money.[87] Although the use of the burgesses in these ways is not so fully described elsewhere, the practice was apparently nothing new, for boroughs had earlier been given allowances in the pipe rolls for sums described as due to default of the moneyers, and the reeves of Lincoln had managed the details of establishing a mint in 1180.[88]

The king first asked burgesses for advice in connection with the issuance of a new coinage in 1248 when the mayor and citizens of London were ordered to elect twelve citizens and to associate with them twelve goldsmiths for giving their advice at the exchequer.[89] Again, when the new gold coinage was planned in 1257, the mayor and citizens of London appeared before the king at the exchequer to answer truthfully whether the new gold coin (worth twenty times the silver penny) would be useful for the common welfare. Even though the Londoners gave a negative answer, with the practical explanation that many men did not have chattels worth even one

86. *C.R. 1247-51*, p. 98.
87. *Ibid.*, pp. 107-108.
88. *P.R. 27 Hen. II*, p. 62; *P.R. 13 John*, pp. 15, 119; *Memoranda Roll 1230-1231*, p. 17.
89. *C.R. 1247-51*, p. 107; F. M. Powicke, *King Henry III and the Lord Edward* (Oxford, 1947), I, 318-321.

gold coin and that the gold would depreciate rapidly with handling, the king decided that the coins would be issued, but he did agree that no one would be required to take them.[90]

Export and import of money also was the concern of some boroughs. In 1279 the king ordered the men of Winchelsea and many other ports to search diligently for silver pieces, clipped money, or other broken silver being carried by any merchants, English or foreign, who were passing through that port. They were ordered to arrest anyone found with these items in his possession, because the king did not want silver taken from the country without special license.[91] In 1283 the mayor and sheriffs of London were ordered to proclaim that no one should accept money in lands overseas on condition of repayment to be made in England, under penalty of forfeiture of his goods in England.[92]

When parliament issued a statute in 1299 concerning false money, it had the following provisions: (1) no one should bring false monies into the kingdom, but all good silver money of whatever realm might be brought to England; (2) no one should sell or barter wool, leather, woolfells, lead, or tin except for lawful sterlings or silver plate assayed and marked at the royal exchange; and (3) no good money or silver should be taken out of the realm without special license. In view of the previous use made of burgesses in this field, it is no surprise to find that the method of enforcement depended upon the services of burgesses. Specifically, the commonalty of each port was to choose two men for whom the electors would be answerable, and these two men with the bailiffs of the port (together called "wardens" in the statute) were to arrest and search all those arriving in their ports. Any men trying to enter England with false money were ordered sent to the

90. *Cronica Maiorum et Vicecomitum*, pp. 29-30.
91. *C.C.R. 1272-79*, p. 518; *Calendar of the Fine Rolls*, I, 106.
92. *C.C.R. 1279-88*, p. 244.

chief royal prison in the county where they had landed, but the money and silver taken from the prisoners were ordered sent to the great exchange. The wardens had to answer at the exchequer for other goods seized from such persons. Furthermore, the statute provided that the wardens were to place a seal upon all sterlings brought into realm and to send men bringing in sterlings to the nearest assayer. If the sterlings were not some of those being counterfeited abroad, the owners were then free to go where they wished; if the money were bad, it was forfeited to the king and the bodies of the owners were in the king's mercy. The other provisions of the statute similarly depended for enforcement upon the wardens, who had to take an oath before the sheriff or chief warden to be faithful in carrying out their duties.[93] Other references show borough officials carrying out these duties, onerous as they might be, with a zeal that led to a damage suit in one case for damaging property by unrolling woolfells in a search for counterfeit money.[94]

Some of the difficulties in enforcing the royal policies on a local level appear in the example of a royal writ containing the order that "pollards" and "crocards," two types of debased coinage, should no longer pass at the value of a full penny, but only for a halfpenny. In consequence of this writ, the officials of London were forced to make a proclamation forbidding Londoners to increase the price of provisions and other items, and the king later supported this policy with a royal writ directed against the same problem on the twenty-eighth of January. A memorandum of February 2 describes the steps taken by the mayor and alderman in calling serjeants of each ward before them to receive instructions about carrying a staff

93. *The Statutes of the Realm* (London, 1810), I, 131-133.
94. *C.C.R. 1296-1302*, p. 266; *Statutes of the Realm*, I, 134; Thomas, *Calendar of Early Mayor's Court Rolls*, p. 41; *C.C.R. 1296-1302*, pp. 480-482; *C.C.R. 1302-07*, pp. 16, 538-539.

so that they would be able to arrest anyone who refused to accept two "pollards" for a penny. Furthermore, such a person should be brought to the sheriff together with the article to be sold.[95] The continuing effort to keep prices from rising appears in a series of prosecutions in the mayor's court against those who violated the policy.[96]

The boroughs proved as useful to the royal administration for the disbursement of funds as they were in the collection of taxes and customs duties or in the enforcement of financial assizes. It is clear from references in the pipe rolls that already in the twelfth century the kings had found a convenient method of making payments for a great variety of purposes by directing borough officials to take these sums from their farms in return for allowances to be made later during the accounting at the exchequer. Customary fixed payments were allowed at the exchequer as a matter of course, but officials of the borough had to produce the royal writs of authorization before the barons of the exchequer would approve an allowance from the farm for any other payments.[97] In view of the advantages to the king of this method of making payments, which allowed him to meet expenses from expected revenues and eliminated awkward transportation of coins as he traveled about the countryside or even as far as the Continent, it is not surprising that the vast number of entries in the various chancery enrolments shows that this method of making payments continued to be used extensively during the thirteenth century. However, it should be noted that none of the payments allowed to borough officials represents a payment by the burgesses from their own funds; the function of officials of the boroughs in these cases was purely one of administration,

95. Sharpe, *Calendar of Letter-Books, Letter-Book C*, pp. 54, 56, 57.
96. Thomas, *Calendar of Early Mayor's Court Rolls*, pp. 59-65.
97. Fitz-Nigel, *Dialogus de Scaccario* (1950 ed.), pp. 87-90. What is said in regard to the sheriff's accounting at the exchequer would apply equally to officials of a borough having the privilege of rendering the account.

making the actual payments and preserving a record for the exchequer account.

The adoption of this method of payment seems particularly natural in providing for the salaries of royal officials whose duties kept them resident within certain boroughs. Such an official was the *contratalliator* who was stationed in Southampton to make a duplicate record of all disbursements made by the reeve on order of the king or the chief justice; his name appears along with that of his son as the recipient of regular payments from the reeves.[98] Similarly we find payments to another royal official, the *talliator vinorum regis,* whose title indicates duties concerned with the entry of wine through the port of Southampton and, probably, with the collection of the king's prize or other customs duty.[99] At London, payments were made regularly to men who had custody of the king's houses at Westminster and of the jail in London, and payments to two of the king's moneyers for establishing a mint appear on an account from Lincoln.[100] Chancery records supplement the allowances on the pipe rolls by giving the orders for payments to royal officials whose salaries had not become a customary allowance from the farm.[101]

By a slight extension of the idea behind these payments the chaplain, gate-keeper, and watchmen of Southampton castle were paid from the borough farm.[102] The men of Newcastle paid the constable of Bamborough castle, the keeper of the king's galley frequently drew payments at Southampton, and the Londoners paid exchequer messengers for delivery

98. *P.R. 33 Hen. II*, p. xxi. The editor cites a description of the functions of the contratalliator "talliare contra prepositum ville de Sudhamtona de liberacionibus factis in eadem villa per preceptum domini regis vel capitalis justic', unde compotus debet reddi ad scaccarium"; *P.R. 31 Hen. II*, 215.
99. *P.R. 14 Hen. III*, p. 201; Cannon, *Pipe Roll 26 Hen. III*, p. 274.
100. *P.R. 26 Hen. II*, p. 58; *P.R. 3 Ric. I*, 136; *P.R. 3 John*, p. 258; *P.R. 14 Hen. III*, p. 97; Cannon, *Pipe Roll 26 Hen. III*, p. 281.
101. *Rot. Litt. Cl.*, I, 39b, 337a; II, 168a, 277b.
102. *P.R. 31 Hen. II*, p. 215; *P.R. 34 Hen. II*, p. 179.

of summonses throughout England in preparation for sessions of the exchequer.[103] Payment by borough officials provided a convenient way to meet the expenses of royal officials, even clerks of the king's own household, as they journeyed through the country in royal service, especially when they met with some delay, such as did the treasury officials who took time to count some money near Winchester.[104] On the accounts of the city chamberlains in Norwich during the years 1293 to 1305, sums paid for the expenses of royal justices are found over and over again, and those for other royal ministers and clerks occur from time to time.[105]

As might be expected, a large number of entries in the records from many boroughs are concerned directly with the expenses of the king, his family, and the court. In 1216 the mayor of Bristol was ordered to take part of the money owed the king as a fine and to pay it out at once for the queen's needs.[106] A visit by the king and his court often seems to have meant that the burgesses were called upon to help meet expenses as exemplified at Gloucester, Lincoln, Northampton, Oxford, Worcester, and York, to name a few.[107] The city of London provided money for the king's expenses on several occasions when he was in the city, and a payment from the London citizens helped finance Henry III's first coronation.[108] In providing supplies and equipment for the household, the role of borough officials in some instances seems to have been limited solely to paying the costs from borough funds, rather

103. John Hodgson, *A History of Northumberland* (Newcastle-upon-Tyne, 1820-58), Pt. 3, Vol. III, col. 142 (from pipe roll 10 Hen. III); *P.R. 33 Hen. II*, p. xxi; *P.R. 34 Hen. II*, p. 180; *P.R. 3 Ric. I*, p. 136.

104. *P.R. 10 John*, p. 127; *P.R. 14 Hen. III*, pp. 97, 200; Hodgson, *History of Northumberland*, Pt. 3, Vol. III, col. 178 (Pipe roll 20 Hen. III); Cannon, *Pipe Roll 26 Hen. III*, p. 281; *Rot. Litt. Cl.*, I, 195b, 401b, 409a, 431a, 453a, 464b.

105. William Hudson and John C. Tingey, eds., *The Records of the City of Norwich* (Norwich and London, 1906-10), II, 31-38.

106. *Rot. Litt. Cl.*, I, 285a.

107. *Ibid.*, pp. 355b, 364b, 386b, 414a, 462b, 502a.

108. *Ibid.*, p. 464a and examples of expenses on pp. 344a, 381b.

than the more usual service of purveyance by taking an active part in obtaining the equipment or supplies. Most entries of this type come from London where the household officials frequently obtained money for the various needs of their departments, such as paying for a cart, supplies, cloth, or a packhorse, to indicate typical payments to the royal pantry, butlery, and kitchen.[109] The wide variety of payments to individuals who had provided some services for the king, the use of writs to borough officials in providing gifts from the king, providing for the expenses of messengers from various foreign powers, and the satisfaction of obligation for fixed alms all show the usefulness of this method of disbursement, which continued throughout the thirteenth century.[110]

Although there can be no doubt of the importance of the boroughs in making disbursements for the king, they were not all equally important, nor did those most important at the beginning of the thirteenth century necessarily continue to be so. During the first part of that century, the development of the chancery brought into existence the records—close rolls and *liberate* rolls primarily—that give evidence from which rough general comparisons can be drawn. The dividing point used is the year 1227, which was selected as the significant year in setting off the administrative improvements of King John's reign and their continuation under the minority of his son from the more fully developed administrative system of Henry III and Edward I. In the early period before 1227, it is already apparent that certain boroughs were being used more than others for making payments in the name of the king. By far the greatest number of payments were made by the officials of

109. *Ibid.*, pp. 408a, 578b; *Rotuli de Liberate ac de Misis et Praestitis, Regnante Johanne*, ed. T. D. Hardy (Rec. Comm., London, 1844), p. 104.
110. *P.R. 1 John*, p. 129; *P.R. 3 John*, p. 258; *P.R. 5 John*, p. 45; *P.R. 8 John*, p. 55; Cannon, *Pipe Roll 26 Hen. III*, p. 257; *Rot. Litt. Cl.*, I, 79a, 234b, 267b, 291a, 383b, 384a, 588a, 604a; *Rotuli de Liberate*, p. 9.

London, but a large number of writs were directed to the officials of Lincoln, Northampton, and Southampton. Probably both the size of the London farm and the location of the city contributed to its value to the royal administration for this purpose. The evidence for this activity becomes especially full with the separate *liberate* rolls, which have been published for the period from 1227 to 1260. For the entire period between 1227 and 1307 the boroughs most frequently used for making disbursements were Southampton, London, and Bristol, ranked in that order according to the number of writs sent to each.[111] Lincoln and Northampton, which had been important in this connection before 1227, were asked to make hardly any disbursements during the remainder of the thirteenth century— with only two writs to Lincoln and five to Northampton during the entire period.[112] The officials of Bristol had made some disbursements for the king in the earlier period, but they became outstanding for this service only after 1227. In addition to the boroughs mentioned above, writs concerning disbursements made for the king were sent during the years 1227 to 1307 to the following: Andover, Cambridge, Canterbury, Chester, Gloucester, Grimsby, Hereford, Newcastle-on-Tyne, Norwich, Nottingham, Oxford, Scarborough, Shrewsbury, Winchester, Worcester, Yarmouth, and York.[113] According to the evidence of the *liberate* rolls and the close rolls, the boroughs were used very frequently in making disbursements during the period from 1241 to 1260, indicating that the procedure had become routine. The separate *liberate* rolls for years after 1260 have not been published, but writs in the later close rolls show

111. An example for each may be found in *C.L.R.*, II, 96; III, 231; Francisque Michel, ed., *Rôles gascons* (Paris, 1885), I, 240b.
112. *C.R. 1259-61*, p. 62; *C.R. 1264-68*, pp. 283-284; *C.L.R.*, III, 254, 326, 377; *C.P.R. 1301-07*, p. 155; *C.C.R. 1296-1302*, p. 545.
113. *C.L.R.*, II, 79, 254, 281, 303; III, 21, 41, 85, 162, 343, 375; *C.R. 1247-51*, p. 548; *C.R. 1261-64*, p. 365; *C.P.R. 1232-48*, p. 431; *C.C.R. 1288-96*, p. 225; *C.R. 1264-68*, p. 323; *C.R. 1234-37*, p. 311; *C.P.R. 1281-92*, p. 70.

that this method of payment, important already in the time of Henry II and even more widely used during the early thirteenth century, continued until the end of the century.[114]

Boroughs also seem to have provided King Henry III with a supply of funds available for emergencies. In 1236 he ordered the bailiffs of Scarborough to collect all the money for which they would normally respond at the exchequer during the Michaelmas term and to deliver it to the king upon his return from Newcastle. Writs of *allocate* would then be issued for that amount.[115] The sheriffs of London were told in 1250 to make payments as directed by two royal officials to redeem furs, cushions, silken cloths, and other things that had been given from the wardrobe as pledges for loans made by Jews and other men in London.[116] Bailiffs of Lincoln and Grimsby in 1260, and of those two boroughs plus York and Chester in 1264, were told to supply money to the king's buyers at the Boston fair because "the king does not have the money at hand for this purpose."[117] When the king was absent on a military expedition in 1266 and had taken his treasure with him, he solved the problem of providing for the sustenance of the queen, who remained at Windsor castle, by issuing orders to the men and community of London to pay her five hundred pounds out of a fine they owed the king.[118] Perhaps the best evidence for the usefulness of these disbursements made by borough officials is the large number of writs that carry such orders, but these few explicit statements serve to re-emphasize this usefulness in a period when the king and his administration were forced to operate without a constant, dependable source of funds.

114. For examples of later entries, see *C.R. 1261-64*, p. 365; *C.P.R. 1266-72*, p. 258; *C.P.R. 1292-1301*, p. 418; *C.C.R. 1272-79*, p. 268; *C.C.R. 1288-96*, p. 225; *C.C.R. 1296-1302*, p. 508.
115. *C.R. 1234-37*, p. 311.   116. *C.L.R.*, III, 271.
117. *C.R. 1259-61*, p. 62; *C.R. 1261-64*, p. 353.
118. *C.R. 1264-68*, p. 187.

Municipal records of London give further insight into the place taken by that city in making disbursements for the king and allow us to follow the give and take of payments and claims for allowances made later at the exchequer. This account rendered by the citizens of London shows the disposition of a large fine amounting to twenty thousand marks, which they had been forced to pay Henry III for their opposition during the Barons' War. From this fine they deducted payments made into the wardrobe by the buyers of the wardrobe and a very large number of other payments made for the king by London officials, so that no money had to be paid into the treasury.[119] A transcript of a letter addressed to the king by the barons of the exchequer on October 31, 1301, contains the statement that the king had ordered an audit of the London account and then gives the results. According to the instructions, allowances were to be made for deliveries, payments, and costs incurred in carrying out orders of both Henry III and Edward I; other deliveries, payments, and costs resulting from a royal order, but not contained in the letters of allowance, were to be listed in a statement sealed with the exchequer seal and sent to the king.[120]

Attorneys for the Londoners appeared at this exchequer audit and presented letters of allowance for about 5,993 pounds; there remained somewhat more than 7,339 pounds to be accounted for. Of this sum, disbursements for 5,000 pounds were placed in view because the Londoners claimed these had been made to the French king by order of Henry III, but the attorneys were unable to produce the royal letters patent ordering such expenditures. Letters of receipt from the French king were

119. Sharpe, *Calendar of Letter-Books, Letter-Book C.*, p. 228. In a case before the King's Council the Londoners charged that the Treasurer had refused to give them credit for some payments. See I. I. Leadam and J. F. Baldwin, eds., *Select Cases before the King's Council 1243-1482* (Selden Society, vol. 35, Cambridge, Mass., 1918), pp. 8-9.
120. Sharpe, *Letter-Book C*, p. 232.

available but no writs of allowances had been sent to the exchequer, even though letters on the patent roll referring to this payment and to a loan of eight hundred marks to Edward promised that an allowance would be made from the London fine.[121] Other payments were not allowed on technical grounds because the attorneys were unable to produce letters of receipt from the men they claimed to have paid. These included payments for fortifying Rochester castle, expenses of a man in royal service, and payments to merchants of Ghent and another man on the king's behalf. Finally, *contrabrevia* for payments to various royal servants for wages and payments for expenses of work on the Tower were still at the treasury, and, for this reason, the exchequer could not act on these payments either.

The next step taken by the London citizens was to present a petition to the king and his council during a parliament held at Westminster in 1302 asking them to approve the allowances for various sums not passed at the exchequer audit. The king and council answered that the payment to the king of France would be allowed because the king's command and the receipt from the French would suffice for a precept, that another payment would be allowed because the king remembered the debt and the fact that it had been paid, and that the treasurer and barons were being instructed to check the accounts of the men who ought to have received other payments as claimed by the Londoners and to allow all payments that could be certified as actually having been made. Writs of *allocate* were duly dispatched on August 23, 1302, to put into effect the allowances granted in this answer to the London petition. In a final action taken on October 1, 1302, a writ was sent to the sheriffs of London ordering them to collect the remainder of the fine for which allowances had not been granted.[122]

121. *Ibid.*, pp. 232-233. For the writ, see *C.P.R. 1258-66*, p. 548.
122. Sharpe, *Letter-Book C*, pp. 234-237.

This one example of payments made by the Londoners for the king is typical of the financial responsibilities of the boroughs as a whole in pointing to the conclusion that the English kings and their ministers had worked out effective ways to turn the growing wealth of the towns to royal profit. Having shown their ability to collect their own farms, the burgesses were encouraged to take an active role in negotiating and collecting taxes, first tallages and later taxes on movables, with negotiations in parliament at the close of the period institutionalizing and centralizing the results of previous experience. Royal control over commerce came to make prominent use of burgesses with a trend from early experimentation to systems regularized by statute, both in the development of a customs system and in the enforcement of coinage regulations.

Wealth in the towns was made even more directly available to the king by the practice of ordering borough officials to make disbursements against the sums due later at the exchequer, a practice that dramatically increased the funds that the king could draw upon at any given time and that made these funds available throughout the year. Should this money due the king be insufficient for his purposes, he could obtain loans either from the burgesses or by their aid to meet the immediate need and thus postpone the eventual accounting, at times almost indefinitely. Because wealth was concentrated in the towns, it is natural that the financial responsibilities should be among the most important administrative responsibilities of the burgesses and take precedence in any discussion of this subject. However, the importance of the boroughs to the royal administration was by no means limited to financial matters but can be proved in various other fields wherever the royal administration sought to make its policies effective on the local level.

CHAPTER IV. THE ADMINISTRATION OF JUSTICE

THAT the ordinary people in medieval England were involved in the administration of justice to a degree unparalleled in the experience of their contemporaries has become almost an axiom of English constitutional history, especially that written since the forceful demonstration of that thesis by Albert B. White. Although his main emphasis was upon the judicial uses of the people through the county juries, his thesis as he stated it would include the boroughs as well:

The thesis is that English kings, working in what they believed to be their own personal interest, so used the English people in government, laid upon them for centuries such burdens and responsibilities, that they went far toward creating the Englishman's governmental sense and competence. . . .[1]

Burgesses certainly were brought directly into the administration of justice in their required appearance before the itinerant justices, an important relationship for administrative work in general, as well as for more narrowly judicial business.

1. *Self-Government at the King's Command* (Minneapolis, 1933), p. 2. However, a warning against exaggeration of the value of this experience is given in Wilkinson, *Constitutional History of England*, III, 23.

Secondly, as a special liberty or franchise, the burgesses took care, in their own borough courts, of judicial business that would have been subject to royal justice in less privileged jurisdictions. In fact, these borough courts might be looked upon as royal courts in an extended sense of that term. This was stated by the author of *Fleta* in describing the different kinds of king's courts in the late thirteenth century:

He has, moreover, his court in the shires, in every county court and in the sheriffs' turns, in hundred courts and in his manors, in the same way as a baron or other freeman, as well as in cities and boroughs, as in the hustings in London, Lincoln, Winchester and York and elsewhere in franchises. . . .[2]

During the course of the thirteenth century, this exempt jurisdiction for the borough courts was widened until the sheriff and other royal officials were forbidden by charter provisions to act within boroughs, always providing the burgesses themselves did not neglect to act.

The responsibility of the burgesses for justice was fixed upon the individual burgess by the tenth section of the Assize of Clarendon as promulgated in 1166:

And within cities or boroughs no one shall have men or shall receive [men] within his house or his land or his soke for whom he will not be sponsor, [guaranteeing] that he will bring them before the justice, should they be summoned, or that they are under frankpledge.[3]

With the introduction of the general eyre, the responsibility became a collective one, for the regular form of summons before the justices provided that twelve burgesses from each borough should appear along with the representatives of the vills.[4] Variations in the number of men necessary are found

2. *Fleta,* ed. H. G. Richardson and G. O. Sayles (Selden Society, 72, London, 1955), II, 110. See also Wilkinson, III, 152.
3. Stubbs, *Select Charters,* p. 171.
4. For an example of the regular summons, see *Rot. Litt. Cl.,* I, 403b. See also *ibid.,* p. 471a; Doris M. Stenton, ed., *Rolls of the Justices in Eyre . . . for Lincolnshire*

in some charters without affecting the basic principle: the burgesses of Colchester after 1189 could acquit themselves by four, at Dunwich the burgesses could name six men to serve with six outsiders in levying a fine in cases involving the borough as a whole, and the citizens of London claimed in 1228 as a custom from the time of Henry II that the articles of the eyre should be delivered to the mayor to answer with the counsel of the elder and more discreet citizens.[5]

However, the administration of royal justice in London was always unusual and not typical of boroughs in general. In the reign of Henry III the mayor and sheriffs were responsible for presenting crown pleas before the king's justiciar at the Tower of London, and it was claimed the practice was customary during the reign of King John and his predecessors.[6] In accordance with this obligation, the mayor and sheriffs were ordered in 1221 to produce all the men who had held the office of sheriff or chamberlain of London since the last time the justiciar had held pleas to answer for any pleas that should have been presented during their terms in office.[7] Except in very rare instances no burgesses were allowed to try crown pleas, but the London aldermen in the twelfth century did have the right to determine in cases of battery or affray with bloodshed whether the case was grave enough to be a crown plea and thus to necessitate the presence of the justiciar.[8]

Lists of amercements in the pipe rolls throw an oblique light upon the responsibility of all boroughs in the later twelfth century in presenting cases before the itinerant justices. Typical entries concern the failure to present a man for selling wine

---

1218-9 and Worcestershire 1221 (Selden Society, 53, London, 1934), pp. 7, 289, 388 *Rot. Litt. Pat.*, p. 129a.

5. *B.B.C.*, I, p. 124; Mary Bateson, ed. *Borough Customs* (Selden Society, 18, 22, London, 1904-6), II, 57.

6. *Rot. Litt. Cl.*, I, 435b; II, 90a, 96b.

7. *Ibid.*, I, 474a.

8. *B.B.C.*, II, lix; Bateson, II, cxlvii.

against the assize, concealment of the unauthorized operation of a mint, non-appearance before the justices, and failure to present crown pleas.[9] At Gloucester the justices amerced the jurors for not presenting all the facts in a case when they neglected to mention that a sword had been found in a house where a robbery had occurred.[10] The burgesses of Colchester, with the exception of four men exempted by name, paid a fine for failing to prosecute malefactors against the Jews.[11] Similarly, payment was made at Cambridge for failing to prosecute a suit as vigorously as should have been done, but in another case the burgesses at York and Cirencester were deemed overzealous and had to pay for false presentation before the justices.[12] It is clear from such entries that the responsibility of presenting cases before the itinerant justices was not an empty formality and meant a real burden, which burgesses were anxious to avoid, as evidenced by fines offered by various boroughs to secure postponement, quittance, or some alleviation of this responsibility.[13]

Even when the burgesses had made their appearance before the justices and presented cases in a satisfactory manner, or had been amerced for their shortcomings, their responsibility was not ended. Next came the task of collecting money to pay for amercements made against the borough as a whole and of collecting the more numerous sums adjudged against individual burgesses; later came the accounting for both types of amercements at the annual reckoning before the barons of the exchequer.[14] An example of the first type of amercement is an

9. *P.R. 22 Hen. II*, p. 57; *P.R. 27 Hen. II*, p. 41; *P.R. 29 Hen. II*, pp. 14, 111; *P.R. 31 Hen. II*, p. 201; *P.R. 32 Hen. II*, p. 8; *P.R. 33 Hen. II*, pp. 65, 139.

10. *PR. 33 Hen. II*, p. 138.

11. *P.R. 6 Ric. I*, p. 36.

12. *P.R. 3 Ric. I*, pp. 66, 95, 114.

13. *P.R. 2 Hen. II*, p. 15; *P.R. 26 Hen. II*, p. 101; *P.R. 29 Hen. II*, p. 116; *P.R. 8 Ric. I*, p. 180.

14. There is some question whether the statement "the burgesses of X render account for pleas" is just a conventional expression. Several entries seem to indicate that the statement is to be taken literally, and other entries that specifically state

entry from the pipe rolls stating that the citizens of Lincoln ought to respond for an amercement of the city for an assault on the Jews.[15] The second is shown when the reeves of Lincoln accounted in 1172 for the pleas before justices William Basset and Alan de Neville and included in their account the names of individuals and the amounts owed.[16] A somewhat longer entry in 1177 lists the reasons for the various amercements as well as the names of individuals.[17] Explicit statement of the part taken by borough officials in collecting such sums was provided in 1242 when the bailiffs of Kingston were named along with the sheriff as having paid the amounts collected from amercements upon individuals. In another case the bailiffs of Colchester reported two shillings from the seizure of chattels from Richard Brodfot to satisfy an amercement against him.[18] This latter action is similar to the provision in the Nottingham charter that the bailiff could levy no distraint upon the house or stall of a reputable man except for a debt owed the king or for a judgment from a crown plea.[19]

A second means by which burgesses were drawn into royal administration of justice, more irregular than duties connected with appearance before the itinerant justices and yet for that very reason more adapted to a variety of uses, was by service on inquisition juries. A few examples will illustrate the variety of purposes for which the king called upon the burgesses as jurors. When the bailiffs of Winchester had determined by inquisition in 1238 that death in a particular case had resulted

---

when the sheriff was accounting for an amercement on a borough give indirect support that the difference in language means a difference in the method of accounting. See for examples, *P.R. 12 Hen. II*, p. 97; *P.R. 13 Hen. II*, p. 150; *P.R. 15 Hen. II*, p. 2; *P.R. 20 Hen. II*, p. 17. Amercements were being reported by burgesses even before the establishment of regular iters; see *P.R. 31 Hen. I*, p. 67.

15. *P.R. 6 Ric. I*, p. 120.
16. *P.R. 18 Hen. II*, p. 95.
17. *P.R. 23 Hen. II*, p. 117.
18. Cannon, *Pipe Roll 26 Hen. III*, pp. 134, 223.
19. Bateson, *Borough Customs*, I, 103.

from an accident, the king pardoned a man arrested on suspicion, who had thereafter fled justice by escaping from a royal prison.[20] In another case involving homicide, the bailiffs of Yarmouth were told to inquire by oath from lawful men in their town about chattels in the possession of a man who had been arrested, and to restore these chattels to the rightful owners.[21] To determine whether six men arrested in 1244 for the death of Simon de Elnestowe were guilty or not, the king ordered the mayor and sheriffs of London to hold an inquisition "according to the custom of the city" in the presence of the king's coroner and, if the prisoners were found guilty, to release them on bail provided by twelve lawful men. A similar inquisition six years later was held to decide whether a writer was guilty of making an attack upon the archbishop of Canterbury; in this case the city officials were explicitly ordered not to free the prisoner if the verdict were guilty.[22]

Inquisition juries seem to have been particularly useful in disputes over property and the seisin of property. Sometimes the problem might consist simply of arriving at an estimate of value, as when King John ordered William Brewer to establish the value of the anchor and ropes of the king's large ship "by view and estimate of the proved and faithful men of Portsmouth who know how much these are worth."[23] Similarly, to find the properties held by the White Monks of Caerleon in 1251 and the value of these properties to the Knights Templars two years later, the mayor and bailiffs of Bristol were associated with the sheriff of Gloucester in an order to hold an inquisition.[24] A royal order to the reeves of Canterbury to ascertain what lands and rents had been held by a certain man preparatory to giving full seisin to his sister as the law-

20. C.R. *1237-42*, pp. 68-69.
21. C.R. *1227-31*, p. 291.
22. C.R. *1242-47*, p. 278; C.R. *1247-51*, p. 165.
23. *Rot. Litt. Cl.*, I, 246a.
24. *Calendar of Inquisitions Miscellaneous (Chancery)*, I, 43, 61.

ful heir probably represents a routine use of the inquisition.[25] Variants of this are the inquiries by the sheriffs of London whether the house formerly held by Aaron Blund, a Jew, before he was disseised actually belonged to the fee of St. Thomas or not, and the task of making an extent of all the property in London belonging to Ralph de Salceto.[26] The citizens of Worcester held an inquisition and assured the king that a purpresture of a parson made on royal land was not a nuisance to the town; permission was that given for the parson to remain in possession for the good of King John's soul.[27] Worth noting because of the scope of the inquiry is a letter patent directed in 1253 "To all citizens, burgesses, bailiffs and other the king's tenants in cities, boroughs, and all other manors and demesnes throughout England" with the order to aid Elerius, abbot of Pershore, who was being sent to make extents and hold inquests by oath of the local men concerning escheats, alienations of escheats, and advowsons of churches and to recall the royal rights to them.[28]

When it came to gathering information or checking on the conduct of officials, the inquisition jury proved its worth time after time in the boroughs and in the counties. An example is the letter of King John in 1206 to the barons of London stating that he had learned the city was suffering from the misconduct of the men responsibile for various tasks, including the collection of tallage, and that he was ordering the election of twenty-four leading men to investigate the charges and to prevent dissent from arising within the citizen body.[29] In 1250 the bailiffs of Gloucester were ordered to hold an inquisition to find the name of the sheriff in office

25. *Rot. Litt. Cl.*, I, 388b.
26. *C.R. 1231-34*, pp. 484, 586.
27. F. W. Maitland, *Select Pleas of the Crown* (Selden Society, 1, London, 1888), I, 96.
28. *C.P.R. 1247-58*, p. 209.
29. *Rot. Litt. Cl.*, I, 64a.

when the queen's apartment was built in Gloucester castle and
to establish the amount that it should have cost, obviously
implying that some tampering with the costs was suspected.[30]
When Peter des Rivaux and his colleagues in the royal household fell from favor in 1234, the local inquiry into misconduct
on their part was carried out in London by the mayor and men
of London.[31] In a more ordinary case the jury dealt with the
question of the amount of a man's debts and whether he was
of sound mind, and in another case with the nationality of
certain merchants.[32] Examples of another important use of the
inquisition to find information for the royal administration
are the letters of *ad quod damnum* concerning proposed construction of various types, and the replies from Lincoln, Newcastle-on-Tyne, Northampton, York, and London.[33]

Supervision of the Jews and gathering of information about
their finances were provided in special instances by local juries
in the boroughs and on a routine basis by answer to similar
questions in the general eyre.[34] Even the suspicion of the Jews
by their Christian neighbors is documented in 1256 with the
appointment of two justices to inquire about the crucifixion
of a Christian boy, and the order to the sheriff of Lincoln
to provide twelve knights and other good men from the county
and twelve men from the city for the jury, in addition to the
mayor, bailiffs, and coroners of Lincoln.[35]

Probably the seriousness of the responsibility placed on
burgesses by service on inquisition juries needs no emphasis,
but two examples may be given that do make this burden ex-

30. *Calendar of Inquisitions Miscellaneous (Chancery)*, p. 32.
31. *C.R. 1231-34*, pp. 581-582; Powicke, *Henry III and the Lord Edward*, I, 137.
32. *C.R. 1247-51*, pp. 262, 523-524.
33. *C.P.R. 1247-58*, p. 652; *C.P.R. 1258-66*, pp. 298, 535; *C.P.R. 1266-72*, p.
260; Sharpe, *Calendar of Letter-Books, Letter Book A*, p. 222.
34. *C.P.R. 1232-47*, p. 228; *C.P.R. 1247-58* p. 64. Questions about Jews are included in the first extant articles for the general eyre of 1194. See Stubbs, *Select
Charters*, pp. 253, 256.
35. *C.P.R. 1247-58*, p. 510.

plicit. Individual responsibility underlies the note recorded in a court roll of 1219 that William, one of the twenty-four of Lincoln, was in mercy because he had contradicted the other twenty-three and was convicted of it.[36] The reaction of the London citizens when the king attempted to extend the scope of the inquisition by a statute of Westminster which required the Londoners to appear outside the city at an inquisition before the king himself was to resist these demands. The Londoners answered a royal summons with the assertion that it was never customary for them to do this and that, therefore, they were returning nothing in answer.[37]

In addition to presenting cases before the itinerant justices, collecting and accounting for amercements, and serving on inquisition juries, the burgesses from the reign of Henry II had to take an active role in the enforcement of royal justice within their boroughs. By the Assize of Clarendon in 1166 burgesses were ordered not only to refrain from hindering the sheriff, but also to help him seize men who had entered the borough and were known to be robbers, murderers, thieves, receivers of such men, outlaws, or men accused under the forest law.[38] Perhaps some entries in the pipe rolls which show allowances for various boroughs "pro iusticiis faciendis per totum annum" are evidence of law enforcement in accordance with this principle, but it is not clear what was done to warrant such an allowance.[39] Fortunately, other references are more explicit.

Officials of the borough, or even the burgesses as a group, were sometimes expected to make arrests on instructions from the king. The reason for ordering officials at Dover, Southamp-

36. Stenton, *Rolls of the Justices in Eyre for Lincolnshire 1218-9 and Worcestershire 1221*, p. 421.
37. Henry T. Riley, ed., *Munimenta Gildhallae Londoniensis* (Rolls Series, London, 1860), II, Pt. 1, pp. 151-155 (Liber Custumarum).
38. Stubbs, *Select Charters*, p. 171.
39. *P.R. 3 Ric. I*, p. 136; *P.R. 1 John*, p. 129; *P.R. 10 John*, p. 33.

ton, Bristol, Portsmouth, and Chester to search carefully for a man and his accomplices who had attempted to assassinate the king and queen and to prevent these men from leaving the country through the ports is obvious.[40] Connection with maritime traffic also explains a letter of King Henry III, who, acting on the request of the king of Scotland, ordered the bailiffs of all English ports to arrest the servants of a Scottish burgess who had taken his ship and goods and were now fugitives at sea.[41] Similarly, the bailiffs of Southampton were notified in 1297 that mariners hired by the warden of Jersey and Guernsey to molest the French had gotten out of hand and seized a ship off Brittany contrary to orders; the bailiffs were expected to arrest the men and to seize the ship when it came to their port.[42] A rather different case, quite exceptional in calling for action outside the borough itself, was provided by the notification to the bailiffs of Norwich in 1267 that many persons who had not yet come into the king's peace after the recent disturbances were setting ambushes for merchants near their city, and the accompanying order that the bailiffs were to take the whole posse of the city if necessary to arrest such persons and place them in safe custody.[43] More far-reaching in its implication in regard to the relation of royal power to the execution of justice in the boroughs was the order sent to the mayor and aldermen of London in 1299 commanding them to arrest, try, and punish persons there who met together either by day or night and spoke ill of the king and his subjects.[44]

The ordinary responsibility of keeping peace within the jurisdiction of the borough is reflected in the decision of the itinerant justices at Oxford in 1285 to place one ward of the city in mercy for not seizing a killer even though the crime had been committed in the daytime and citizens were obli-

40. *C.R. 1237-42*, p. 146.   41. *C.P.R. 1258-66*, p. 287.
42. *C.C.R. 1296-1302*, p. 140.   43. *C.P.R. 1266-72*, p. 272
44. *C.P.R. 1292-1301*, p. 403.

gated to seize him.[45] The burgesses of Bridgnorth protested the assertion of the sheriff's bailiffs and the men of the country that the burgesses had the duty of following the trail of stolen cattle through their town, on the grounds that this was impossible, and they claimed their being forced to pay forty shillings for failure was unjust; the outcome of the case is not recorded.[46] When the mayor of Northampton attempted to obtain pledges for the appearance of a man before the justices in eyre in 1229, the man refused and the mayor was forced to arrest him when ordered to do so by one of the justices. Because this seizure went contradictory to a decision previously made in a church court, the dean of Northampton placed the borough under an interdict, and the mayor found how hard performance of his duty to the king could be.[47] The bailiffs of Norwich were brought strictly to account for neglecting their duty when royal serjeants were beaten in Norwich in their efforts to protect the Jews. The bailiffs were ordered to report what justice they had dispensed in the case (as they were bound to do in preserving the king's peace), but they made no answer to the charge.[48]

Among the remaining responsibilities of burgesses in the execution of justice that of answering for the chattels of a felon seems most prominent. Different cases show that officials of the borough had to answer to royal officials whether the accused felon had fled and taken sanctuary, or had been arrested and executed, and such responsibility may have been incumbent upon them without special mandate from the king.[49] In 1298 when asked to certify why they had taken land

45. J. E. Thorold Rogers, ed., *Oxford City Documents Financial and Judicial 1268-1665* (Oxford Historical Society, XVIII, Oxford, 1891), p. 195.

46. Maitland, *Select Pleas,* I, 113.

47. F. W. Maitland, *Bracton's Note Book* (London, 1887), II, 291.

48. H. G. Richardson and G. O. Sayles, eds., *Select Cases of Procedure without Writ under Henry III* (Selden Society, 60, London, 1941), p. 23.

49. *P.R. 16 Hen. II,* p. 79; Doris M. Stenton, ed., *Rolls of the Justices in Eyre Being the Rolls of Pleas and Assizes for Gloucestershire, Warwickshire, and Staf-*

into the king's hand, the bailiffs of Scarborough replied that the owner had behaved well in their town but had been hanged by the king's foresters. That the bailiffs had acted on their own initiative is shown by the royal reply that this was not to be regarded as conviction for a felony and that they were not to intermeddle with the messuage further if this was their only reason for doing so.[50] Borough officials were also responsibile for taking such things as boats and horses as *deodand* due the king in cases of accidental deaths within their jurisdictions.[51] The mayor and bailiffs of Oxford aided the enforcement of royal justice in 1279 when they took security from a prisoner for the fine he had made for killing a buck in the forest.[52] Entries from a Gloucester court roll show the bailiffs taking care of minor details in the administration of justice; the perils of helping to enforce royal justice were experienced by a London sheriff who had to overcome resistance in one case and found himself being sued in another for trying to carry out his duty; and the presence of clerks as students at Oxford brought special problems for the harassed officials of that borough.[53]

The transfer of land and other kinds of royal property within boroughs was an especially important part of the execution of justice by borough officials. When these officials received a royal mandate to grant seisin to a particular individual, the responsibility for executing the king's wishes in the matter

fordshire, 1221-1222 (Selden Society, 59, London, 1940), pp. 559-560; *C.R. 1227-31*, p. 173; *C.R. 1231-34*, pp. 167, 171, 493; *C.R. 1253-54*, p. 286; *C.C.R. 1302-07*, p. 259; *Liber Quotidianus Contrarotulatoris Garderobae*, ed. John Topham (London, 1787), p. 4.

50. *C.C.R. 1296-1302*, p. 184.

51. Doris M. Stenton, ed., *Rolls of the Justices in Eyre Being the Rolls of Pleas and Assizes for Yorkshire in 3 Henry III (1218-19)* (Selden Society, 56, London, 1937), p. 296; *C.R. 1231-34*, p. 397; *C.R. 1227-31*, p. 159; *Pat. R., II*, 176.

52. *Calendar of the Fine Rolls*, I, 108.

53. Stenton, *Rolls of the Justices in Eyre for Gloucestershire, Warwickshire, and Staffordshire, 1221, 1222*, pp. 123, 130-131; Thomas, *Calendar of Early Mayor's Court Rolls*, p. 36; *C.R. 1231-34*, pp. 568, 570; *C.P.R. 1232-47*, pp. 218-220.

and for giving actual possession of the land or property rested with the local officials. This action seems to have been an essential step, important enough legally that a claimant in a royal court could cite seisin given by borough officials as a precedent which was co-ordinate in authority with a royal order.[54] Liberties of a borough sometimes made necessary the close co-operation of the sheriff with the mayor and bailiffs of the borough in bringing a case involving land to final decision before the itinerant justices.[55] These liberties held by many boroughs were identical with or similar to the provisions in the London charter of 1155: "Concerning their lands and tenures within the town, right shall be done to them according to the custom of the city."[56] When decisions made in borough courts in regard to seisin were called into question, the procedure seems to have been to have the bailiffs and four men of the borough bring the record to the king's court and vouch for it.[57] In one case in which the seisin granted by the bailiffs of Southampton in executing a royal writ was questioned, the borough court declared in favor of the seisin, and this judgment was upheld in the king's court.[58] Nevertheless, individuals could bring cases against seisin granted by borough courts before the king by charging that a false judgment had been made, and the final determination of the seisin would then be made in the royal court.[59]

Since transfer of property was often the final act terminating a great variety of royal business, grants of seisin by the

54. The defendant in a Lincolnshire case in 1219 claimed he had seisin "per breue domini Regis et per consideracionem maioris et aliorum civium Lincolnie. . . ." Stenton, *Rolls of the Justices in Eyre for Lincolnshire 1218-9 and Worcestershire 1221*, p. 399.
55. Maitland, *Bracton's Note Book*, II, 230-232.
56. *B.B.C.*, I, 134-135.
57. *Curia Regis Rolls*, VIII, 297; IX, 60; Doris M. Stenton, ed., *The Earliest Lincolnshire Assize Rolls A.D. 1202-1209* (Lincoln Record Society, 22, n.p., 1926), p. 41.
58. *Curia Regis Rolls*, I, 50.
59. *Ibid.*, IX, 60.

burgesses involved them indirectly in all kinds of business, important and trivial alike. In 1228 the king sent a letter close to the mayor and sheriffs of London ordering them to give full seisin of certain property to Hubert de Burgh, the justiciar; four years later, with a change in Hubert's political fortunes, the king ordered the same officials to give full seisin of all these lands and rents to Peter des Rivaux, a leading household official.[60] Apparently a mandate by King John to the bailiffs of Dunwich and several royal officials in 1217 represents the unusual circumstances resulting from rebellion against him, for men who had returned to allegiance were having their properties restored to them.[61] Most letters ordering grants for seisin were less dramatic, involving such things as a normal inheritance, correction of an injustice, execution of a judicial decision, or that ambiguous phrase expressed by transferring property as "gifts of the king."[62]

Often the boroughs were called upon to keep royal prisoners or assume other administrative duties in regard to such prisoners, and allowing royal prisoners to escape brought a fine to more than one borough.[63] Temporary use of the borough jail at Worcester for prisoners of the sheriff was ordered by the king in 1231 because the castle jail had become dilapidated; in 1259 the mayor and sheriffs of London were asked to keep all prisoners arrested by the sheriff of Essex in Newgate prison because he had no jail.[64] The mayor and sheriffs of London in 1234 were ordered to remove the irons from several prisoners and to see that they did not lack for food while in Newgate prison; such expenses for food for prisoners were regularly allowed from the city farm when an accounting was made at

---

60. *C.R. 1227-31*, p. 21; *C.R. 1231-34*, p. 112.
61. *Rot. Litt. Cl.*, I, 332b.
62. *Ibid.*, pp. 60b, 104b, 197a, 205a, 259a, 294a, 321b, 458a.
63. *P.R. 26 Hen. II*, pp. 7, 146; *P.R. 27 Hen. II*, p. 63; Hodgson, *History of Northumberland*, Pt. 3, Vol. III, col. 258 (from the pipe roll 45 Hen. III).
64. *C.R. 1227-31*, p. 567; *C.R. 1256-59*, p. 387.

the exchequer.[65] An interesting series of entries in the *liberate* rolls for 1242 shows that outlaws taken as royal prisoners on the island of Lunday were first held by the bailiffs of Bristol, then some of these were delivered to London by a man who was paid out of the Bristol farm, and finally they were kept by the mayor and sheriffs in Newgate and Fleet prisons, where they were still imprisoned four months after their capture.[66] Part of the activities of burgesses were due to the necessity of keeping men who appeared as approvers before royal courts, arming them, and transporting them to the places of trial.[67]

A dispute occurred in London in 1300 when the king sent a writ commanding the mayor and sheriffs of London to produce certain prisoners at Gloucester in answer to charges made against them by an approver there. The mayor answered that he did not have custody of a prison in London, and that he should not have to answer for prisoners because that was not part of his duties. The sheriffs answered that some of the prisoners were free London citizens and had been released on bail for appearance at the first assize held at the Tower or before royal justices for delivering Newgate prison. The sheriffs were willing to deliver other prisoners placed in their custody by the marshal of the king's household to any place in London but not outside, unless the king issued a writ of allowance for the cost of delivering them elsewhere. The dispute ended with a memorandum in the municipal account to the effect that the mayor and aldermen did not wish the sheriffs to suffer loss on account of this answer to the king, and they promised to indemnify them before the king if necessary.[68]

65. *C.R. 1231-34*, p. 423; *C.L.R.*, III, 40.
66. *C.L.R.*, II, 138, 148.
67. *P.R. 3 Ric. I*, p. 136; *P.R. 3 John*, p. 258; Cannon, *Pipe Roll 26 Hen. III*, p. 283; *Rot. Litt. Cl.*, II, 46a, 56b, 108a; Doris M. Stenton, ed., *The Earliest Northamptonshire Assize Rolls A.D. 1202 and 1203* (Northamptonshire Record Society, V, Lincoln and London, 1930), p. 116.
68. Riley, *Munimenta Gildhallae Londoniensis*, II, Pt. 1, pp. 133-135 (*Liber Custumarum*).

Although most of the tasks that fell to the borough in the administration of justice were undertaken by the usual borough officials, some officials within the borough were specifically elected to perform duties in this field. The usual title for such an official elected in a borough to act for the king in judicial matters was "coroner," but men who performed similar functions in other boroughs were known as justiciars. In the royal charter granted to Northampton in 1200 provision was made for the election of four leading burgesses as coroners to keep the pleas of the crown and to manage other royal business within the borough. According to the charter provisions, these four men were also expected to act as a check on the reeves to see that they treated both rich and poor alike in the execution of their official duties.[69] Similar provisions were included in the charters granted in 1200 to the burgesses of Shrewsbury, Lincoln, Gloucester, and Ipswich, but a second charter granted to Shrewsbury five years later provided that only two men be elected coroners.[70] Fifteen more boroughs received the right to elect coroners by charters granted during the thirteenth century, and Bedford also had such a right, as shown by royal letters in 1248 and 1250 ordering the bailiffs to have a full court assembled for electing a new coroner in place of a man who had died.[71] The burgesses of Chester were granted the unique privilege in their charter of trying crown pleas and receiving the amercements from such trials.[72]

Additional information concerning the election of coroners is given in other chancery records. A letter close to the sheriff of Lincoln in 1218 gave notice that the king had ordered the

69. B.B.C., I, 246.
70. Ibid., p. 247.
71. C.R. 1247-51, pp. 93, 260.
72. B.B.C., II, 146, lxiv. Rolls of such crown pleas may be found in R. Stewart-Brown, Calendar of County Court, City Court and Eyre Rolls of Chester, 1259-1297 (Chetham Society, n.s. 84, Manchester, 1925), p. 152 for 1287-88 and in A. Hopkins, Selected Rolls of the Chester City Courts (Chetham Society, 3rd ser., II, Manchester, 1950), p. 29 for 1316.

mayor and proved men of Lincoln to elect four men of that city as coroners for keeping crown pleas. The next step was to present the elected coroners to the sheriff, who would administer an oath requiring them to perform their duties faithfully. A short note addressed to the mayor and men of Lincoln follows the letter to the sheriff in the rolls.[73] A contemporary description of the election of coroners at Ipswich gives an insight into the actual proceedings within a borough when the burgesses put into effect the privilege of electing coroners as granted by a charter. In the election at Ipswich, two of the four men chosen to be coroners were already bailiffs of the borough. All four coroners took oath after their election "to keep the pleas of the crown and to care for other matters that pertain to the crown in the same borough and to see that the aforesaid bailiffs justly and lawfully treat both rich and poor," but the possibility of the coroners actually interfering with the bailiffs was undoubtedly remote in view of the interlocking nature of the two offices after the election.[74]

An official styled "justiciar" in Henry I's charter to London performed functions similar to that of the coroner in other boroughs. The justiciar was elected by the citizens of London to keep crown pleas and to plead them in London. However, the clause granting the right to elect the justiciar was not included in later charters of the city.[75] The charter for Colchester granted in 1189 also provided for an elected justiciar to keep and to plead crown pleas.[76] In 1219 it was provided before the itinerant justices that twelve burgesses of Stamford were attorned in place of the coroners to keep crown pleas and the attachments pertaining to the crown in that borough.[77]

73. *Rot. Litt. Cl.*, I, 364b.
74. Gross, *The Gild Merchant*, II, 116-117.
75. *B.B.C.*, I, lxxxvii, 242.
76. *Ibid.*
77. Stenton, *Rolls of the Justices in Eyre . . . for Lincolnshire 1218-9 and Worcestershire 1221*, p. 416, case 864.

Like the county coroner, the presence of the borough coroner was necessary at the eyre where both officials delivered rolls concerning cases within their jurisdictions.[78] Such records provide an example of the Oxford coroners at work in 1296 in a case arising when a clerk was found dead in the hostel where he lived. When the coroner viewed the body, he found a large knife wound, explained later at an inquest as having been inflicted by other clerks in a fight over a woman.[79] In another case from 1298, Edward Hales was indicted before the coroner for killing a man and placed in jail, but he escaped and fled to a church for sanctuary. There he admitted his guilt before another coroner and abjured the realm; his goods were seized to be given to the Hospital of St. John in accordance with a charter of Henry III as confirmed by Edward I.[80] Failure by the coroner of Norwich to act in a case had to be carefully explained before the justices on eyre and the explanation confirmed by the jurors.[81] In 1264 a confessed killer presented himself before the coroners and bailiffs at Norwich, who arrested and imprisoned him; the coroners added a note in their roll that the bailiffs would answer for the prisoner.[82] When the bailiffs of that city took matters into their own hands in 1285 and hanged a man, instead of presenting him before the itinerant justices after an inquest had been taken, the king revoked the liberties of Norwich and did not restore them until four months later and at the cost of a permanent increase in the farm there.[83]

The administration of justice in the Cinque Ports was unusual because the Ports had a common court where even crown

78. Charles Gross, *Select Cases from the Coroners' Rolls A.D. 1265-1413* (Selden Society, 9, London, 1896), p. xxviii.
79. *Ibid.*, p. 87.
80. Rogers, *Oxford City Documents*, p. 151.
81. Hudson and Tingey, *Records of Norwich*, I, 200.
82. *Ibid.*, p. 207.
83. *Ibid.*, pp. 220-221.

pleas were presented. This common court, known as the Shepway, was a recognized institution as early as 1150, but it was only during the course of the thirteenth century that the organization was perfected. As a royal court, the Shepway was useful because it served as a connecting link joining the Cinque Ports to the central government in matters of administration and control. While the warden of the Cinque Ports, a royal appointee, served as president of the court, the decisions of the court were made by officers from the various ports sitting as judges. In 1321 the court was said to have met regularly once a year, but it could always be called by the warden either on his own initiative, by royal mandate, or on appeal from one of the ports.[84]

During the thirteenth century, the chief business settled at the Shepway by the jurors from each port was connected with the articles of the eyre. Legal disputes arising out of maritime traffic also were a frequent concern of the court.[85] A letter of summons sent to the various Ports in 1227 enumerates some of the articles to be answered when the bailiffs and twenty-four barons of each port appeared at the Shepway before the itinerant justice, Martin de Pateshull. The first item of business was the presentation of crown pleas—those not completed when the court last met and new pleas arising since that time. Furthermore, inquiry was to be made concerning those who were in the king's mercy but had not yet been amerced and concerning churches in the king's mercy. Finally, a general order was given to the bailiffs of the Ports to present all other pleas and attachments that should come before the court at Shepway, in order that they might be decided according to the laws and customs of the kingdom.[86] Another

84. K. M. E. Murray, *The Constitutional History of the Cinque Ports* (Manchester, 1935), pp. 60-62.

85. *Ibid.*, pp. 63, 65.

86. *Rot. Litt. Cl.*, II, 213b. The civic use of the title "baron" in England was confined to London and the Cinque Ports. Since there is no evidence of this title

letter was sent to the bailiffs of Yarmouth, a borough with which the Cinque Ports were constantly at odds, to inform them of the meeting at the Shepway and urging any burgess of Yarmouth who wished to present a complaint to appear at that session of the court. A copy of this letter was also sent to the bailiffs of Dunwich offering the men of that borough the same opportunity to lay their complaints before the itinerant justice if they wished.[87]

Other boroughs did not enjoy the rights exercised by the courts of the Cinque Ports, but constitutional developments during the thirteenth century did make the borough increasingly independent. By 1260 most of the English boroughs had a *non-intromittant* clause in their charters, which provided that no sheriff or other royal official could intermeddle with any plea or matter pertaining to the town, except for default of the burgesses themselves and saving to the king his crown pleas.[88] Furthermore, about the middle of the century, many boroughs obtained the privilege of the return of writs, described by Tait as "the right to execute the precepts of royal writs, which would have been done by the sheriff."[89] Three boroughs had this privilege before 1256, and some seventeen more had received it by January 18, 1257.[90]

The examination in the preceding pages of the practice in administering justice contains examples from both before and after these charter provisions and shows that burgesses had been exercising some judicial functions during the previous half century before these charter provisions greatly extended borough jurisdiction. On the other hand, the independence of

in any of the Ports except Hastings before 1206, Tait concluded that the usage was associated with a closer union and increased importance of the Cinque Ports after the loss of Normandy. See Tait, *Medieval English Borough*, pp. 256-260.
87. *Rot. Litt. Cl.*, II, 214a.
88. *B.B.C.*, II, 155-159.
89. *Ibid.*, p. lxi.
90. *Ibid.*, pp. 171-172.

the boroughs from royal jurisdiction can all too easily be over-emphasized if one is content to concentrate on charters and legal relationships. In fact, having received such jurisdictional privileges in their charters, the burgesses were forced to assume new responsibility for carrying out the policies of the royal administration in judicial and other matters within the borough; thus the borough and its officials became in practice a branch of the royal administration on the local level. Since the middle of the twelfth century, the kings had sometimes used boroughs as if this were the case, but only with the grants of these jurisdictional privileges is there explicit recognition of the situation.

The close interconnection of the borough and the monarchy is shown by the relationship developed between borough courts and royal courts. Liberties of a borough were sometimes pleaded in royal courts to claim that cases had to be tried within the borough, and cases raised in royal courts in opposition to such liberties were at other times dismissed subject to trial by the borough.[91] Execution of the assizes of *novel disseisin* and *mort d'ancestor* within the boroughs varied according to the practice in individual boroughs on the question whether these writs applied to tenements within the boroughs or whether citizens should go to their own borough court in such disputes.[92] When the bailiffs of a borough failed to carry out the orders of a sheriff in cases referred to them from his jurisdiction, they were called to account before the king's court, where they at times successfully claimed their liberties to show that such cases should be tried by borough custom, and other times they asserted such liberties; whether successfully or not cannot be determined from the court rolls.[93] In at least one

91. *Curia Regis Rolls*, I, 138; IX, 370; Doris M. Stenton, ed., *Pleas before the King or His Justices 1198-1202* (Selden Society, 67-68, London, 1952-53), I, 178.
92. Stenton, *Pleas before the King*, I, 387.
93. *Ibid.*, II, 104; *Curia Regis Rolls*, II, 70; Sayles, *Select Cases in King's Bench*, II, 51.

borough, Ipswich, the burgesses were willing to give three marks to the king in 1203 in order that the assize of *novel disseisin* of tenements in Ipswich would be tried in the borough.[94] Similarly, the burgesses of Derby gave one mark for the right to execute justice on William the approver, whose conviction and sentence to be hanged would normally have been executed by royal officials.[95] Perhaps royal control was not entirely abandoned in cases surrendered for trial in the boroughs, for in two cases transferred to the city of Chester by Edward I the royal directive was so explicit that little was left for the city court to do except carry out orders.[96]

However, the superior jurisdiction of royal courts might also be used to support the authority of borough courts. When the bishop of Worcester infringed upon the liberties of the borough there in trying a thief before his court, the citizens brought a case against him in a royal court.[97] In a jurisdictional dispute with an abbot, the bailiffs of Chester planned to obtain a writ in the king's name if the king were willing to support them on the issue.[98] Failure of the tenants of a powerful order like the Hospitallers to fulfill their civic obligations was corrected by a royal court, presumably after local efforts by the borough court had been ignored by the defendants.[99] On the other hand, in spite of the liberty of boroughs to try cases other than crown pleas within their own courts, the party dissatisfied with such a decision could still appeal to royal courts by a writ of false judgment, and the determination of error not only brought a reversal of the decision made by the borough court, but also meant a fine for that court.[100] Similarly, royal power

94. Stenton, *Earliest Northamptonshire Assize*, p. 134.
95. *Curia Regis Rolls*, III, 89.
96. Stewart-Brown, *Calendar of Court Rolls of Chester*, pp. 5, 24.
97. *Curia Regis Rolls*, IX, 353.
98. Stewart-Brown, *Calendar of Court Rolls of Chester*, pp. 152, 156.
99. Maitland, *Select Pleas of the Crown*, I, 97.
100. Sayles, *Select Cases in King's Bench*, I, 63; *Curia Regis Rolls*, VI, 290; Wilkinson, *The Constitutional History of England*, III, 162.

was asserted just as strongly when the burgesses defaulted in carrying out their responsibilities in administering royal justice. It is clear, therefore, that however much liberty a borough might have, such claims could not stand against the king himself, for the sheriffs were ordered to execute the royal commands where borough officials had failed to act.[101]

Brought into the expanding judicial system of Henry II in the later twelfth century, the borough became an important link in the administration of justice. Most boroughs never escaped the responsibility of presenting crown pleas before the itinerant justices, but by the second half of the thirteenth century borough courts were handling other judicial business as prescribed by the charter privileges of *non-intromittant* and return of writs clauses in their charters. This expanded jurisdiction of the borough court did provide training for burgesses in handling their own affairs, as pointed out by Professor White, and any temptation to shirk the additional responsibility involved was blocked by the close supervision of the borough court by royal courts. By the late thirteenth century, borough courts had become for all practical purposes a local manifestation of royal justice, and the author of *Fleta* was only being realistic when he wrote of them as the king's courts in the boroughs.

101. *Curia Regis Rolls,* IX, 166; X, 286.

CHAPTER V. MILITARY AND
NAVAL RESPONSIBILITIES

THE naval contribution of burgesses in the seaports was far more important than support given the army, for burgesses not only provided ships for the navy, but they also exercised a general control over shipping in support of royal military policy. After the loss of Normandy in 1204, the need for both ships and supplies for cross-Channel expeditions increased, and the military role of the burgess became more important than before. As for support of the armies, it was in providing equipment and supplies that the burgesses played a significant part. When the various ancillary military functions are added to the balance, it becomes clear that the overall value of the borough to the military strength of the English kings in this period was considerable, and that the naval contribution was indispensable.

For the later twelfth century the pipe rolls contain almost no evidence of participation by burgesses in direct combat, but these rolls do supply ample documentation of their importance in providing military supplies. Despite this lack of information concerning combat, there can be no doubt that burgesses could be called upon for defensive service, at least, if the need arose. The Assize of Arms in 1181 provided that each burgess, like any other free man, was to have a padded surcoat, an iron cap, and a lance; any additional arms in the possession of the burgesses at the time of the assize were to be redistributed in some way that would be of service to the king.[1]

This principle of military service by burgesses was kept alive throughout the thirteenth century, with occasional evidence of actual fighting. After the loss of Normandy, the elaborately organized plans for the defense of England provided for one or more constables in each borough to lead the men of the community in preserving the peace of the realm; all men over twelve years of age were bound by an oath to this service.[2] More informative are letters from King John in 1212 which call for a general levy from townships and boroughs to provide armed men and horses for a crossing to the Continent in the king's service. On the fifteenth of June, these letters were dispatched to many boroughs ordering that various numbers of the "proved and better men" be ready for royal service as follows: Canterbury, 40; Dover, 20; Rochester, 20; Kingston, 10; Chichester, 40; Winchester, 40; Southampton, 20; Wallingford, 10; London, 100; Colchester, 40; Hertford, 10; Norwich, 20; Yarmouth, 20; Cambridge, 20; and Huntingdon, 20.[3] The same expedition was probably the reason for a letter to Northampton on the twenty-fifth of August in which the reeves and proved men of that borough were ordered to appear with horses, arms, and the town militia at Fotheringay to aid the king in any way that Hugh de Neville should command.[4]

1. Stubbs, *Select Charters*, p. 183, arts. 3, 4, and 6.
2. Gervase of Canterbury, *Gesta Regum* in *The Historical Works of Gervase of Canterbury*, ed. *William Stubbs* (Rolls Series, London, 1880), II, 97.
3. *Rot. Litt. Cl.*, I, 130b. Patricia Barnes in her introduction to *P.R. 14 John*, p. xxii, points out that the number of men required is equal to the knight service lost from Normandy.
4. *Rot. Litt. Cl.*, I, 122a.

The practice of having all the men in the boroughs take an oath to bear arms continued during the thirteenth century. In 1230 the bailiffs and barons of the Cinque Ports were commanded to take the oath in the same manner as they had done in the time of King John.[5] The following month, the king sent three men to organize the *jurati ad arma* in Kent, and arms of various types based on the amount of chattels a man possessed were required of everyone in Kent, whether he lived inside or outside a borough, city, or town. Furthermore, several men were appointed as constables in each city or borough—the number depending upon the size of the place—to summon the *jurati ad arma* without delay and to make lists of all the men who had been sworn within each district for the defense of the realm.[6] In 1253 the Assize of Arms was renewed with orders for each sheriff to administer the oath to men from fifteen to sixty years of age in cities and boroughs, as well as outside of them. This time it was provided that the ordinary borough officials would command their men instead of special officials chosen for the purpose. Associated with this command was a renewal of the organization for watch and ward; every borough should have twelve men, and every city six men for each gate, to stand watch during the entire night throughout the period from the Ascension to Michaelmas. Any outsider trying to enter the borough or city was to be arrested, and, if he proved to be suspicious, he was to be kept in custody until he could be turned over to the sheriff.[7] Finally, the Statute of Winchester in 1285 put this same responsibility for arms and watch and ward in a form that lasted more than three centuries.[8]

Some of the letters enrolled at the chancery for this period

5. *C.R. 1227-31*, p. 395.
6. *Ibid.*, p. 398.
7. Stubbs, *Select Charters*, pp. 363-364.
8. Sir Maurice Powicke, *The Thirteenth Century* (Oxford, 1953), pp. 53-54; *Statutes of the Realm*, I, 97.

give evidence of direct participation by burgesses in military campaigns. In 1231 the burgesses of Marlborough paid a fine of five marks to avoid the military service ordered in a summons to join the royal army in Wales.[9] Two years later, the bailiffs of the ports were ordered to guard the seacoast and prevent the crossing of Richard Suhard' and Warin and Philip Basset.[10] A letter close of 1243 refers to "great labors" performed by the men of Dunwich in guarding the coast.[11] When the king sent John de Grey as commander of the defensive forces in 1263 against the king's enemies in Wales, the mayor, bailiffs and other proved men of Hereford were ordered to aid him. Also, the king ordered the farm of Hereford for the next term of the exchequer given to Grey for this service.[12]

During the civil warfare in 1264 and 1265 between supporters of the king and the supporters of Simon de Montfort, both parties used the chancery machinery at times to secure military support from various boroughs. Such use makes it clear that the boroughs had an obligation for military service, but the details of participation by burgesses in the various military plans of both sides were dependent upon the extraordinary circumstances of the period and by no means provide typical examples of military obligations of the boroughs. When an invasion from the French mainland by the friends of Henry III was momentarily expected during the months from July 1264 to late autumn, the boroughs had an important share in guarding the coast for Simon de Montfort and the barons who controlled the king.[13]

In late July 1264, Earl Simon and the earl of Gloucester marched to the west to put down depredations being made against the English in Wales, and the burgesses at Shrewsbury,

9. *C.R. 1227-31*, p. 542.   10. *C.R. 1231-34*, p. 326.
11. *C.R. 1242-47*, p. 90.   12. *C.R. 1261-64*, p. 203.
13. *C.P.R. 1258-66*, p. 361; *C.R. 1261-64*, pp. 364, 409; Powicke, *King Henry III and the Lord Edward*, II, 476.

Gloucester, and Hereford were ordered to give them assistance[14] During the period of Simon de Montfort's ascendancy, several boroughs received orders to help secure castles for new constables appointed by the earl; these orders were usually sent in the king's name, although one was attested by Simon himself and the whole council.[15] Many boroughs were ordered to aid in opposing the king's supporters, who finally landed in England in May 1265.[16]

The burgesses of Shrewsbury wrote a letter to the king about 1266 asserting that, together or individually, they were prepared to safeguard the faith they owed the king even to danger of the spilling of blood and death and that the borough's defenses had been strengthened to further this purpose. However, in view of the loss of trade and the impoverishment of the burgesses during the great war in Wales, they asked to be exempted from paying the remainder of their tallage.[17] After the defeat of Simon de Montfort, the burgesses at Lynn were ordered in 1267 to aid royal officials being sent there to protect the town and sea coast.[18] The men of the Cinque Ports were also used in preparations to suppress rebels still holding out in the Isle of Wight.[19]

Edward I ordered the citizens of London to aid in the defense of the coast in 1296 when trouble with France seemed imminent. In an assembly to consider the reply to the royal writ dated March 15, 1296, three men were outspoken in their opposition to the royal order to send armed men on horseback with the king's son to Kent, but they later changed their minds and agreed to go themselves. On April 9 Edward wrote again

14. *C.P.R. 1258-66*, p. 363.
15. *Ibid.*, pp. 373, 383, 392.
16. *C.R. 1264-68*, pp. 121, 122; *C.P.R. 1258-66*, p. 423.
17. Walter W. Shirley, ed., *Royal and Other Historical Letters Illustrative of the Reign of Henry III* (Rolls Series, London, 1862-66), II, 310-311.
18. *C.P.R. 1266-72*, p. 130.
19. *Ibid.*, p. 142.

to notify the Londoners that the warden of London and other men named would tell them the royal will on the subject. The answer given by the citizens was that they had sent forty men with horses, fifty crossbowmen, and footsoldiers to aid the king's son at the coast. Some days later, the Londoners apparently agreed to send twenty more horsemen to the seaports for four weeks and to provide each man with twenty marks for expenses. This money was taken from the tax granted previously from the boroughs to the king in parliament on November 27, 1295.[20] In a letter patent dated April 22, 1299, the king granted the citizens of London that their coming with horses and arms to the maritime parts of Kent and Sussex for defense of the coast as a voluntary service should not prejudice their city in the future.[21]

Much more important than this direct military service were the various activities of the burgesses in support of the royal army. The role of the borough as a source of military supplies is already well documented in the pipe rolls for the twelfth century, and more information is found in both exchequer and chancery records for the thirteenth century. Most of the references in the pipe rolls consist of allowances from the farm of the borough in payment for the supplies and thus indicates that the function of the burgesses was to provide the supplies at the expense of the king, rather than to bear the cost of such supplies themselves.

Some examples will illustrate this type of reference. The account of London on the pipe roll for 1193 contains a list of supplies sent to the army: rope, iron, leather, and other materials for a siege engine; stones, rope, quarrels, shields, sulphur, and some other items requisitioned by a royal writ; and thirteen ells of green cloth and seven fur hoods given to seven

20. Sharpe, *Calendar of Letter-Books. Letter-Book C,* pp. 23-24; Riley, *Munimenta Gildhallae Londoniensis,* II, Pt. 1, pp. 72-76 (*Liber Custumarum*).
21. *C.P.R. 1292-1301,* p. 409.

knights who were taken into the king's service.[22] Three years later the burgesses of Shrewsbury provided supplies for the army and paid carpenters to build ships for carrying troops.[23] In 1211 the Londoners received an allowance, and they also supplied military equipment for the royal galley in preparation for an expedition to Ireland.[24] Henry III ordered a large canvas tent to serve as a pavilion or audience hall while engaged in a campaign against France in 1228, and the London account contains the detailed list of expenses for this tent.[25] In 1260 the men of Carlisle supplied salted fish to the army in Wales and received an allowance at the exchequer.[26]

The initial step in military preparations is given in the chancery letters that supplement such references as these in the pipe rolls. In 1218 the mayor of Lincoln was ordered immediately upon receipt of the royal command to provide two hundred pickaxes and one thousand ropes to be used for mangonels and other siege engines.[27] Three years later, a letter to the mayor of Lynn carried the royal command to provide ropes for the same purposes, and required further that two men from Lynn accompany the shipment to testify concerning the cost of the ropes, which the king had promised to repay.[28] Letters close directed to the bailiffs of Northampton on several occasions in 1224 required them to provide the following men and equipment: ten uncured cow or horse hides or twelve tanned hides to make slings for siege engines, two saddlers with their equipment to strengthen shields, fifty strong pickaxes, and nine hundred quarrels for crossbows.[29] The reeves of Southamp-

22. *P.R. 5 Ric. I,* p. 158.
23. *P.R. 8 Ric. I,* p. 42.
24. *P.R. 13 John,* p. 132.
25. *P.R. 14 Hen. III,* p. 97 and pp. xxv, xxvii.
26. F. H. M. Parker, ed., *The Pipe Rolls of Cumberland and Westmorland 1222-1260* (Cumberland and Westmorland Archaeological Society, extra ser., XII, Kendal, 1905), p. 191 (from pipe roll 43 Hen. III).
27. *Rot. Litt. Cl.,* I, 365b.
28. *Ibid.,* p. 448b.
29. *Ibid.,* pp. 606b, 612a, 615a, 640a.

ton provided cables for raising heavy timbers and cords for mangonels in 1215.[30] In 1214 John ordered the mayor of Winchester to have all the shields in the city prepared and delivered to a royal minister for transportation to the king in Picardy.[31] In preparation for a campaign by Henry III in 1227, the bailiffs and proved men of Winchelsea and of Rye were ordered to proclaim throughout their towns that all merchants selling foodstuffs should come with grain and other necessary foodstuffs to Portsmouth, where the king and his army would pay well for provisions.[32] Many borough officials received letters in 1297 and again in 1301 commanding them to induce merchants who sold food and other necessities to take their wares to Berwick-on-Tweed for sale to the royal armies assembling there.[33]

The citizens of London were outstanding in their service to the royal administration in furnishing military support to the king by carrying out all kinds of tasks previously mentioned. A single letter close of 1221 in the form of a writ of *computate* directed to the barons of the exchequer in favor of the London sheriffs lists allowances for the following military services: seventeen shields sent at the king's need, six pence paid to carters for transporting two mangonels from London to the army, three shillings six pence allowed for expenses of serjeants who supervised the transport of the mangonels, one cart load of ropes sent to the army, horses and equipment provided for two master carpenters accompanying the mangonels, a half mark used for the expenses of the carpenters, equipment provided for carrying the king's money, various pieces of mili-

30. From a fragment of a close roll printed in *Memoranda Roll 10 John*, pp. 135, 139.
31. *Rot. Litt. Cl.*, I, 207a.
32. *Ibid.*, II, 211a.
33. *C.C.R. 1296-1302*, pp. 77, 489-490; Sharpe, *Calendar of Letter-Books. Letter-Book C*, p. 91. Payments to burgesses for military supplies are shown in a wardrobe role, but any administrative activity in regard to these supplies seems to have been carried out by wardrobe officials. See Joseph Bain, ed., *Calendar of Documents Relating to Scotland* (Edinburgh, 1884), II, 365.

tary equipment transported for the royal forces, other mangonels removed from the crypt of St. Paul's in London and
transported as the king had ordered, and eight pairs of hand-
cuffs provided for the use of prisoners captured by the royal
forces.[34] In one letter concerned with similar military supplies,
the king ordered them to be sent with an armed escort of
London citizens, and further specified that a clerk should accompany the shipment to take care of the necessary accounting
for an allowance to be made at the exchequer.[35]

References to the place of the borough in providing military
supplies for royal armies are frequent for the years 1241 to 1260,
especially in the published *liberate* rolls, and are found again
toward the end of the century in the close and patent rolls. A
large number of these references in the *liberate* rolls are concerned with the purchase and delivery of military supplies by
the citizens of London, with items supplied being hauberks,
habergeons, quarrels, a horse and equipment, and shields.[36]
The *liberate* rolls also contain entries for Newcastle-on-Tyne,
Bristol, Hereford, Shrewsbury, and Southampton; entries from
the close rolls after the last published *liberate* roll add Bridgnorth, Gloucester, Lynn, Portsmouth, Scarborough, Winchester, and York to the list.[37] On the whole, the chancery
evidence for the later thirteenth century seems to indicate that
the boroughs were not so important as sources for military
supplies as they had been early in that century, but no definite
conclusion can be reached without an examination of the unpublished *liberate* rolls after 1260. In the available records, only
London seems to have continued to be quite important in this
connection.

34. *Rot. Litt. Cl.*, I, 450a.
35. *Ibid.*, p. 605b.
36. *C.L.R.*, II, 26, 173, 187, 189, 244, 246.
37. *Ibid.*, II, 260, 262, 268, 314; III, 45, 141; IV, 69; *C.R. 1227-31*, p. 596;
C.R. 1231-34, p. 317; *C.R. 1242-47*, p. 216; *C.R. 1253-54*, p. 61; *C.C.R. 1302-07*,
pp. 120, 188.

Some orders from the king to borough officials directed them to have arms made for the royal forces. In 1215 King John ordered the reeves of Canterbury to have all the workmen in their city work day and night (*de die et nocte*) making pickaxes; they were to deliver the weapons to Rochester immediately when finished.[38] At Northampton, all men who knew how to work at a forge were put to work making four thousand quarrels for crossbows, and other men feathered these missiles; a similar order to the bailiffs of Oxford specified six thousand quarrels.[39] A rather lengthy series of entries at Gloucester was concerned with payments from borough officials to men who were manufacturing quarrels for the king's crossbowmen. In 1230 the bailiffs were ordered to make the same payments to William de Malemort for this work as they had previously made to his brother John; the rate listed in this entry was six pence and one obol for a day's production amounting to a hundred quarrels.[40] By the end of the month William was receiving an extra penny per day and had been provided with an unskilled helper or apprentice.[41] Entries concerning the wages of these men at Gloucester continued on an average of two per year in the *liberate* rolls from 1240 to the final printed roll in 1260.[42] An entry from the close roll for 1265 orders a payment to John de Malemort, who was making quarrels in Gloucester castle, apparently continuing a family occupation.[43]

Sometimes the supplies demanded from the boroughs were for garrisons of various castles rather than for armies in the field, and at other times the burgesses provided money or

38. *Rot. Litt. Cl.*, I, 231b.
39. *Ibid.*, p. 638a.
40. *C.R. 1227-31*, p. 362.
41. *Ibid.*, p. 364. The roll is defective, but the provision for someone "qui capit in die duos denarios et obolum" may be for an apprentice.
42. The earliest reference noted was in *C.L.R.*, II, 1 (1240); the last is *C.L.R.*, IV, 226 (1255).
43. *C.R. 1264-68*, p. 157.

materials for the construction or repair of such strongholds. A typical order, except for the mention of military service, is a writ to the mayor and proved men of Oxford in 1215 telling them to aid a royal official in providing the castle at Oxford "with arms, foodstuffs, stone, timber, and all necessities, even with your bodies if need be."[44] During the same year, the reeves of Winchester and of Southampton were ordered to deliver their farms to William Brewer for supplying the castle at Winchester, instead of paying the money at the exchequer in the ordinary way.[45] After an important battle in the Barons' War at Lincoln, the reeves of that city were ordered to make payments to the sheriff for repairs to Lincoln castle on two occasions in 1218.[46] Other boroughs receiving writs for strengthening castles were Bristol, Canterbury, Colchester, Gloucester, Hereford, Hertford, London, Northampton, Scarborough, Southampton, and Winchester. [47] It is perhaps an indication of a stronger royal control of internal affairs that only a very few of these entries come from the later thirteenth century, in no way comparing to the number from the reign of John and the minority of his son.

Certain entries from Marlborough and Newcastle-on-Tyne are more interesting than the usual type because the men of those boroughs were required to take an active role in overseeing construction work on royal castles. In addition to a routine letter commanding the bailiffs of Marlborough to pay a hundred shillings from their farm for construction work at the royal castle, a second letter ordered that the bailiffs and proved men of the borough should assign two men to the constable for viewing the work done there and for reporting to the king

44. *Rot. Litt. Cl.*, I, 198a.
45. *Ibid.*, p. 227a.
46. *Ibid.*, p. 356a.
47. *Ibid.*, pp. 5a, 199a, 231a, 276a, 418a, 492b, 529b, 576a; II, 44b, 62a, 131a, 140a; *C. R. 1242-47*, p. 303; *C.R. 1251-53*, p. 73; *C.R. 1259-61*, p. 380; *C.R. 1256-59*, p. 336; *C.R. 1264-68*, p. 307.

about it.[48] In 1221 the bailiffs of Newcastle were ordered to select a proved man from their town to serve along with a second man chosen by the sheriff from outside the town in viewing and reporting on the work being done on the royal castle by the constable.[49] These examples have the special value of showing that the king and his household officials considered the town bailiffs a regular part of the local administration to be relied upon even for providing a check on important royal officials.

More important to the miltary defense of the realm than aid given in building and supplying castles were the walls of the boroughs themselves. This was recognized by the king and his ministers who took an active interest in the fortification of boroughs during the early years of the thirteenth century. A continued interest was evidenced during the reign of Henry III by widespread grants of murage, a term defined by Ballard as "a toll on certain commodities granted by the King for a specified time to assist the burgesses of any borough in fortifying that borough. . . ."[50] Not surprisingly, Edward I also favored the construction of strong fortifications around boroughs.

As early as 1204 King John ordered the citizens of Chichester to enclose their city for their own security and the king's benefit; the execution of this mandate was insured by the provision that the bishop of Chichester should view the work and that the sheriff of Sussex should have the power to distrain burgesses with the bishop's orders.[51] That such walls were actually considered to the royal interest—John's words were not so much rhetoric—is indicated by the circumstance that the burgesses at Shrewsbury were allowed to deduct from their farm in 1212 payments they had made in walling their

48. *Rot. Litt. Cl.*, I, 588b.   49. *Ibid.*, p. 452a.
50. *B.B.C.*, I, xlix-l.   51. *Rot. Litt. Pat.*, p. 45b.

town.[52] A military purpose also probably explains a letter in 1215 to the mayor and proved men of Exeter ordering them to have all houses removed if they were on the walls, over the ditch, before the barbican, or otherwise detrimental to the city.[53] During the same year the king granted to the burgesses of both Colchester and Stafford the right to take timber near their boroughs for enclosing and strengthening them; a recently discovered fragment of the close roll for that year contains the order for the enclosing of Stafford.[54]

In a short letter that is a forerunner of later grants of murage, the king in 1216 granted the proved men of Hereford for the purpose of enclosing their town the right to collect a toll from the goods carried into it on packhorses—a toll which had already been collected at their gates, but apparently not by the burgesses themselves.[55] Three years later, Henry III granted them the right to collect tolls at all their gates for a period of three years to be used in walling their town, as they were accustomed to take them when Engelard de Cygoing was the bailiff of King John.[56] In 1218 the burgesses of Shrewsbury were ordered to proceed with all diligence in strengthening and enclosing their town so that no harm should come to them or to the royal interests through their neglect and so that no enemies of the king might gain entrance to their borough.[57] Another type of royal aid is shown by the notification sent in 1220 to the sheriff of Shropshire stating that the king had allowed the burgesses at Bridgnorth to take some tree trunks and old oaks from the royal forest for use in walling their town.[58]

52. *P.R. 14 John*, p. 90.   53. *Rot. Litt. Cl.*, I, 268a.
54. *Ibid.*, pp. 193a, 199b; *Memoranda Roll 10 John*, p. 136.
55. *Rot. Litt. Cl.*, I, p. 267b.   56. *Pat. R.*, I, 224.
57. *Ibid.*, p. 169. Tait cited this example as the first order of its kind in England, but no special tolls are mentioned and there seems to be no other significant difference between it and the few earlier references cited above, even that of Chichester in 1204. See *B.B.C.*, II, lxviii.
58. *Rot. Litt. Cl.*, I, 421b.

With the year 1220 regular grants of murage begin to appear in the patent rolls. On the twenty-sixth of June the burgesses of Shrewsbury and Bridgnorth received a four-year grant of murage according to the following schedule for enclosing their towns: one obol for every cart from Shropshire and one pence for every cart entering from outside the county, one farthing for every packhorse loaded with goods for sale except for loads of wood, one obol for every horse or cow brought for sale, one pence for hogs or fowls if as many as ten were sold but only one obol if five were sold, and four pence from each shipload of goods coming to Shrewsbury for sale. The sheriff of Shropshire was ordered to proclaim throughout the county the terms of this grant and to cause it to be observed.[59] Within a month after the grant by the king, difficulties arose when the bailiffs demanded payments from the master of the Knights Templars, and the king dispatched a letter to the bailiffs ordering them to postpone their demands until further orders from the king, and to return anything that might have been seized in connection with those demands.[60]

Throughout Henry III's minority grants of murage were made to numerous other boroughs, and both Shrewsbury and Bridgnorth were granted several extensions of their privileges. Other boroughs receiving grants of murage during this period were Exeter, Gloucester, Hereford, Lincoln, Northampton, Oxford, Scarborough, Stafford, Worcester, and York.[61] The terms of the grant to Scarborough differed from those to other boroughs, but only in the schedule of tolls. All these grants of murage are known from letters recorded either on the patent or close rolls, but in 1224 the king granted the earliest charter

59. *Pat. R., I,* 238-239.
60. *Rot. Litt. Cl., I,* 423b.
61. *Pat. R.,* I, 426 (Worcester, 1224), 459 (Stafford, 1224), 473 (Hereford, 1224), 495 (Exeter, 1224), 499 (Northampton, 1224), 508 (Scarborough, 1225), 518 (Lincoln, 1225); II, 32 (York, 1226), 61 (Gloucester, 1226), 62 (Oxford, 1226).

known to have included an authorization for collecting murage.[62]

During the years 1227 to 1307, at least twenty-nine boroughs were granted the right to take murage at some time. Only the years between 1240 and 1250 show practically no grants in effect. In 1261 some eighteen boroughs had such grants; in 1305 sixteen boroughs currently had that privilege. Usually royal grants allowing boroughs to collect murage were valid for only relatively short periods, but frequent renewals made it possible for many boroughs to collect this toll over long periods. Exeter had the right to collect murage for twenty-three years with renewals after 1285, and Newcastle-on-Tyne possessed the right for twenty-two years consecutively after 1265.[63] Exemptions, such as those granted to the Knights Templars and the Hospitallers, may have reduced the revenues actually obtained from this toll somewhat; certainly the chancery was forced to issue numerous letters ordering local officials to honor such exemptions.[64]

Certain other records give some information about the walling of towns. In 1253 the citizens of Norwich obtained a royal license to enclose their town and to construct nine gates that could be guarded in time of war. However, when the people of the county complained at the sheriff's tourn that the city had disturbed the common roads, the sheriff sided with the persons bringing the complaint and amerced the city. The men of Norwich then pointed out in a petition to the king that the wall was "to the benefit of the king and for the greater security of the town," and asked for a remedy against the unjust conduct of the sheriff.[65] A practical recognition of the value of borough fortifications to the royal administration is provided by a

62. Ballard, *English Borough in the Twelfth Century*, p. 16.
63. These figures are based on grants of murage found in the *Patent Rolls*.
64. A series of exemptions from murage is given in *C.R. 1247-51*, p. 534.
65. Hudson and Tingey, *Records of Norwich*, I, 59.

letter close of 1263 granting the burgesses of Northampton the farm due from their borough at Michaelmas to close and repair their walls for the security of the king and themselves.[66]

Another military responsibility of the boroughs, even though a minor one, was the safe custody of hostages and prisoners. Several letters written by King John deal with this subject, including a letter patent issued in 1202 directing all bailiffs of English seaports wherever royal prisoners should land to provide those from Poitou with a safe conduct and reasonable supplies for reaching London.[67] In 1217 the advisers of Henry III experienced some difficulty when they tried to get the barons of the Cinque Ports to release prisoners they had taken during the fighting with Louis of France, even though a truce had been signed with France.[68]

A later series of references deal with Welsh prisoners being kept in the Tower of London. In 1242 the sheriffs of London were commanded to find reasonable sustenance for Griffin, son of Llewelyn, and other Welsh prisoners.[69] Later entries refer to the costs of keeping this important royal prisoner and his companions; expenses were allowed for bedding, brushwood and coal, a tablecloth, canvas, sheets, a counterpane, a frying pan, a mortar, dishes and cups, towels, and funeral expenses of Griffin's son.[70] In 1244 the sheriffs were ordered to receive Oweyn, another son of Griffin, and five other Welsh prisoners to be delivered by the constable of the Tower, and to transport them under a safe escort to Lichefeld, where they were to be turned over to the justice of Chester.[71] Furthermore,

66. *C.R. 1261-64*, p. 241.
67. *Rot. Litt. Pat.*, pp. 16b, 129a, 131a-b; *Rot. Litt. Cl.*, I, 180b.
68. *Pat. R.*, I, 96, 129.
69. *C.L.R.*, II, 147.
70. *Ibid.*, pp. 160, 161, 171, 189, 199; Michel, *Rôles gascons*, p. 254b; Cannon, *Pipe Roll 26 Hen. III*, pp. 282-283.
71. *C.L.R.*, II, 252.

London officials were expected to choose three good foot-cross-bowmen in their city and three serjeants for escorting the Welsh prisoners to Chester. When these men arrived in Chester, they were to stay in the royal service under the command of the justice at Chester, and the sheriffs of London were responsible only for providing money for their expenses on the way to Chester.[72]

In July 1304 the king ordered hostages from Bayonne kept in safe custody by the burgesses of York, Nottingham, Shrewsbury, Bristol, Oxford, Northampton, Winchester, and Stamford. The royal order also specified conditions for the safekeeping of these hostages. While it was ordered that they should be kept in such a manner that they would be unable to escape, no chains were to be used and they were to be permitted to move about in the borough under good custody.[73] In April 1304 the burgesses of Oxford and Shrewsbury received an order to surrender the hostages under their custody to the sheriffs of their respective counties for delivery to London at the next exchequer proffer.[74] That such responsibility for keeping hostages was not to be taken lightly was shown when the mayor and bailiffs of Winchester were ordered in 1305 to send six men to the king's court to answer for the escape of a hostage and to receive the judgment that the court would make in the case.[75]

A final contribution made by burgesses to royal armies was the payment made by borough officials to soldiers, sometimes companies of mercenaries encamped near the boroughs but more often the garrisons of nearby castles. Examples of such payments have been collected for the following boroughs: Bamborough, Bristol, Carlisle, Hereford, London, Newcastle-on-Tyne, Portsmouth, Scarborough, and Southampton.[76] The

72. *Ibid.*, p. 253.   73. *C.C.R. 1302-07*, p. 215.
74. *Ibid.*, p. 258.   75. *Ibid.*, p. 317.
76. Madox, *History and Antiquities of the Exchequer*, I, 384 n. (from Memoranda Roll 6 Hen. III); Hodgson, *History of Northumberland*, Pt. 3, Vol. III, col. 276

fullest information comes from Newcastle beginning in 1221 with a series of letters close numbering from two to five each year with orders to the bailiffs to make payments from the farm to crossbowmen stationed there and in Bamborough castle. From the figures given in these letters—total payments, number of crossbowmen, per diem rate of pay, and length of time paid—it can be shown that these payments provided the only source of wages for these men over an extended period of time.[77] However, such regular payments did not mean that the burgesses of Newcastle might not be asked to make other occasional payments for military purposes, such as the wages of a foot serjeant for forty days and a much larger sum to the constable for keeping Bamborough castle.[78]

Evaluated from the standpoint of the burgesses, the support they gave royal armies was more important than their naval responsibilities, because support for armies might be expected from any or all boroughs, whereas only the boroughs that were ports were involved with the navy. Nevertheless, from the viewpoint of the royal administration the naval contribution was more valuable. Indeed without the boroughs there would have been no English navy in the twelfth and thirteenth century, for even such ships and galleys of his own that the king had were usually constructed, outfitted, cared for, and manned by men from the ports, and these royal vessels were never more than a small part of a fleet in royal service. Consequently the gathering of a fleet for the king was accomplished only by the dispatch of batches of letters from the chancery and a great amount of hard work by local officials in the ports where they were received.

(from Pipe Roll 51 Hen. III); Cannon, *Pipe Roll 26 Hen. III*, p. 283; *Rot. Litt. Cl.*, I, 152a, 160a, 236a, 279a, 503a, 590b, 608a; II, 88a, 102a; *C.L.R.*, I, 11.

77. One of the entries is *Rot. Litt. Cl.*, I, 462b; Hodgson, Pt. 3, Vol. III, cols. 127, 130 ff. (from Pipe Roll 5 Hen. III with annual accounts following).

78. *Rot. Litt. Cl.*, I, 510b; II, 129a; *C.L.R.*, I, 12.

Naval responsibilities incumbent upon the ports can be divided into two broad spheres of activity: first, providing ships for the king's use; and, second, impressment of merchant ships for royal service. The best-known obligation of boroughs in providing ships for the king's service was that of the Cinque Ports, but the importance of the fleet from the Cinque Ports should not be overemphasized. For one thing, the king could also rely upon his own ships and merchant ships which could be impressed for naval service. Furthermore, in the early years of the thirteenth century, the organization of the Cinque Ports provided only a loose bond among them, and their naval activities more often resembled those of pirates than the activities of a national fleet.[79] During the invasion by Louis of France, the Cinque Ports supported Louis some of the time and were generally unreliable in their allegiance at other times; it was not until February 1217, four months after John's death, that the Ports came over to the English cause. A battle fought by twenty vessels from the Cinque Ports against a French fleet of more than twice that number near Sandwich on St. Bartholomew's Day (August 24) in 1217 probably marks the first time that the vessels of the Cinque Ports acted as a unified fleet with an established plan of action. Even so, the division of spoils after the battle serves as a reminder of the selfish motives that continued to influence their actions.[80]

Because the Cinque Ports did not render accounts at the exchequer, their naval contribution in the later twelfth century must be sought in other records. A charter granted to Hastings by King Henry II some time within the first three years of his reign provided that the burgesses were to send twenty ships into the king's service for fifteen days annually at their own expense, and that any additional service was to be

79. Murray, *Constitutional History of the Cinque Ports*, pp. 2-3; F. W. Brooks, *The English Naval Forces 1199-1272* (London, [1932]), pp. 79, 95.
80. Murray, pp. 35-36.

paid in full by the king. When Rye and Winchelsea were added
to the Cinque Ports by Richard I, their charters specified they
were to provide two ships to make up the twenty that were
due from Hastings.[81] By an odd chance, the pipe rolls do provide the earliest reference to the collective fleet of the Cinque
Ports and to the Ports themselves as a collective body. When
Gervase of Cornhill was ordered in 1184 to account for arrears
from Kent for the period when he had been sheriff, he explained that he had spent the money in 1173-74 in time of war
as a payment for the ships of the Cinque Ports.[82]

The loss of Normandy in 1204 gave the Cinque Ports an
increased importance as the first line of defense against a
hostile coast, and they retained an important position reaching
the height of their power during the reign of Edward I, even
though the ultimate result of losing Normandy was to decrease
their role because the period for which they owed service was
too short in relation to the long, time-consuming distances for
sailing to Gascony.[83] Despite the trouble these men gave the
king by their piratical raids and private feuds with other English ports, the naval service they owed the king was important
enough that in 1278 Edward I confirmed an earlier charter
granted the Cinque Ports in 1260, instead of penalizing them
for recent disturbances.[84] The ship service had been regularized
to fifty-seven ships annually at the expense of the Ports for
fifteen days when summoned by the king, and an investigation
in 1295 revealed the same obligation for fifteen days not including time spent in reaching the scene of operations or the
time for returning.[85] Allowance for wages of men from the
Cinque Ports when they stayed more than fifteen days in royal
service is shown in a letter close of 1305 directing the treas-

81. *B.B.C.*, I, 90.   82. *P.R. 30 Hen. II*, pp. 135-136.
83. Brooks, p. 88.   84. Murray, p. 29.
85. *B.B.C.*, II, 115; John E. Morris, *The Welsh Wars of Edward I* (Oxford, 1901),
p. 106.

urer and barons of the exchequer to audit the accounts. Wages were owed for a crossing to Gascony, for bringing grain to Gascony, and for service in Scotland; on their side of the account, the Ports owed one thousand marks as part of their fine for the fifteenth of 1290, and two thousand as a fine for the fifteenth of 1296.[86]

During the thirteenth century, the office of Warden of the Cinque Ports developed into a permanent one with authority over the Cinque Ports; after the Barons' War this office was in the hands of the constable at Dover. This change provided a channel of communication with the Ports bringing them more closely into the general organization of the country, and it gave the Ports a new unity making possible an effective administration of the Ports as a whole.[87] With the development of this office, more administrative responsibility fell upon the warden, who was a royal official and usually a leading magnate of the realm, and the administrative duties left for the Portsmen themselves were of a secondary order. For the purpose of the following discussion of naval responsibilities, only those royal letters addressed directly to the barons themselves have been used, because they alone provide unequivocal evidence of responsibility by the burgesses, as opposed to the responsibility of the bailiffs or the warden, who were primarily royal officials.

The early years of the thirteenth century during the reign of John and the minority of his son saw a great deal of naval activity, with the Cinque Ports being called upon to provide their ship service both as a group and as individual ports. In June 1202 the barons of the Ports were informed that the king had learned that the king of France planned to ship food to his army by sea, producing a threat that was to be met by the

86. *C.C.R. 1302-07*, p. 278.
87. Murray, pp. 77-78.

Portsmen guarding the seas and the king undertaking to see that no food, or at least very little, would be allowed to reach the army by land.[88] Routine orders for the owed service from the Cinque Ports were issued in that year, 1204, and 1213.[89] In 1206 when the king was preparing a large army and fleet in an attempt to regain his lost possessions on the Continent, he renewed the charters of the Cinque Ports as an apparent move to strengthen their loyalty to him.[90]

After the battle of Sandwich in 1217 where the ships of the Cinque Ports played a decisive role against the French, a letter patent was issued to express the king's gratitude and to announce that two barons of the Ports were being sent to oversee the distribution of the spoils among the participating vessels.[91] Later in the year the ships from the Ports were again summoned, but this writ is chiefly notable for the terrible consequences threatened if they should fail to obey the royal mandate.[92] Three letters in 1224 and 1226 show the dependence of the royal administration upon the fleet of the Cinque Ports for controlling the Channel Islands, with the Ports being ordered to aid the warden of the islands whenever he needed to call upon them.[93] During these years 1224 to 1226, the Cinque Ports took an important part in the struggle by the English to maintain a foothold against the French on the Continent, especially during the last two years when the war was carried on mainly by the naval forces of either side. Not only were the ships used, but King Henry III and his ministers repeatedly asked the barons of the Cinque Ports for their advice in naval planning, according them the status of experts both for guarding the coasts and curbing the activities of captains who raided commerce almost at will.[94]

88. *Rot. Litt. Pat.*, p. 15a.
89. *Ibid.*, pp. 9b, 38b, 106b.
90. Brooks, p. 89.
91. *Pat. R.*, I, 88.
92. *Ibid.*, p. 89.
93. *Ibid.*, p. 455; II, 34.
94. Brooks, pp. 148, 183; *Pat. R.*, I, 503; II, 25.

The fame of the Cinque Ports should not be allowed to obscure the fact that other English boroughs along the coast were required to send men and ships for the royal navy throughout the thirteenth century. In 1205 King John gathered a fleet at Portsmouth and raised a large expeditionary force preparatory to an attempt to regain lost territories on the Continent, but his barons refused to follow the king abroad and the expedition was a complete failure.[95] The bailiffs of the ports in eleven counties were ordered by the king in 1208 to force the ships of the Cinque Ports to come to England for royal service, and the men of all the ports were required to list the ships of their own ports for going into the king's service.[96] Similar orders for collecting ships and making lists were sent to various ports in 1211, 1213, 1214, 1226, and 1227.[97] The need of ships for both fighting and transportation of troops to the Continent was met by ships from the Cinque Ports and other boroughs throughout the thirteenth century, with letters being sent out every two or three years to some ports until the 1260's.[98] Naval service of a different type was involved in 1266 when Yarmouth, Lynn, and Ipswich were specifically mentioned among the ports of Norfolk and Suffolk ordered to pursue men from the Cinque Ports who were disturbing the king's peace.[99]

Expeditions into Wales also required the services of a fleet provided by the Cinque Ports in 1258, and that group and other boroughs at later times.[100] There were twenty-five ships

95. P.R. 7 John, pp. xii, 131, 256; Rot. Litt. Cl., I, 33b.
96. Rot. Litt. Pat., pp. 80a, 85a.
97. P.R. 13 John, p. 2; Thomas Rymer, ed., Foedera, revised by Adam Clarke and Fred Holbrooke (London, 1816), I, pt. 1, 117; Rot. Litt. Cl., I, 177b; II, 150a, 151a, 205a, 211a.
98. C.R. 1227-31, pp. 207, 232, 294; Pat. R., II, 397; C.R. 1231-34, p. 319; C.P.R. 1232-47, pp. 44, 92, 125, 187; C.L.R., II, 65; C.R. 1237-42, pp. 455, 456, 467, 495; C.P.R. 1232-47, pp. 293, 400; C.P.R. 1247-58, pp. 230, 234, 363; C.R. 1251-53, pp. 239, 243, 355, 466, 471, 474; C.R. 1253-54, p. 110; C.R. 1254-56, p. 8; C.R. 1261-64, pp. 168-181.
99. C.P.R. 1258-66, p. 653.
100. C.R. 1256-59, p. 297.

from the Cinque Ports and one from Southampton in the royal fleet for 1277, and forty ships and two galleys from the Cinque Ports in 1282; in each expedition the crews received wages from the king for about two months' service beyond the period of owed service.[101] A general order for the assembling of a fleet at Winchelsea was given in April 1297, and ships from the Cinque Ports, Yarmouth, Southampton, Portsmouth, Dunwich, Ipswich, Bristol, Lynn, Grimsby, Scarborough, Bamborough, Newcastle-on-Tyne, and Chester were ordered to be on hand.[102] Loss of his ship by one of the burgesses from Scarborough resulted in a case before the King's Bench when the bailiffs and proved men failed to compensate him according to custom, even though he had gone into royal service on behalf of the whole community.[103] Later in the year a letter addressed to the Cinque Ports alone ordered them to assemble their ships at one of the Ports because the truce with France was about to expire.[104]

An order issued in December 1298 for the assembly of ships at Carlisle in preparation of an expedition against Scotland was deferred twice and finally postponed indefinitely, with the understanding that the ships might be required at any time on a forty days' notice.[105] Expenses for service by the Cinque Ports in 1299 were paid by the wardrobe, and chancery entries give further evidence of ships assembled for expeditions against the Scots in 1301, 1302, 1303, and 1306.[106] The commission of Gervase Alard in 1306 provided that he was to be the captain and admiral of the ships from the Cinque Ports and all other ports westward from Dover to Cornwall; another man named Ed-

101. Morris, *Welsh Wars of Edward I*, pp. 106-107.
102. *C.C.R. 1296-1302*, pp. 100-102.
103. Sayles, *Select Cases in King's Bench*, III, 67-69.
104. *C.P.R. 1292-1301*, p. 325; *C.C.R. 1296-1302*, p. 191.
105. *C.C.R. 1296-1302*, pp. 290, 307, 313, 374-375.
106. *C.P.R. 1292-1301*, p. 583; *C.C.R. 1296-1302*, pp. 482-483, 612; *C.C.R. 1302-07* pp. 76, 78, 433; *C.P.R. 1301-07*, p. 131; *Liber Quotidianus Contrarotulatoris Garderobae*, pp. 167, 271-273, 275.

ward Charles had charge of the ships from the mouth of the Thames north to Berwick-on-Tweed.[107] The order given a royal clerk to investigate the men of the Cinque Ports and certain other ports who failed to observe a summons in 1306 provides an indication that such naval service was not popular with the burgesses themselves, and the designation in another record of two men to punish those who did not send men or ships in accordance with the quotas agreed upon reinforces this impression.[108]

The second method for providing ships for the royal navy was by even more sweeping mandates ordering the impressment of all merchant ships that should enter English ports. Such a directive probably had the twofold purpose of preventing ships from reaching the enemy and of strengthening the English fleet.[109] The responsibilities of borough officials is illustrated in a letter patent of May 15, 1224, addressed "to all bailiffs and to the barons of the Cinque Ports" with an endorsement at the end listing some twenty-eight ports where copies were sent, many of which would qualify as boroughs. The king announced that the truce with France had expired at Easter and ordered the bailiffs to retain all vessels in their ports and to prepare them for the king's service. He further commanded that no ship carrying merchandise or other cargo should leave port without a special order, and that all ships belonging to foreigners should be arrested upon arrival in English ports.[110] The purpose in seizing all merchant ships can be found also in orders to the bailiffs of seaports to retain the large ships for transporting knights and their horses and the smaller for transporting supplies, and in orders of another type

107. *C.P.R. 1301-07*, p. 438.
108. *Calendar of the Fine Rolls*, I, 540; *Rotulorum Originalium*, I, 121.
109. Brooks, *English Naval Forces*, p. 170.
110. *Pat. R.*, I, 483.

specifying that one certain ship or a group of ships from those seized in the ports be sent to the king.[111]

During the period of enforcing such general orders for impressment of merchant ships, the inevitable accompaniment seems to have been a rash of chancery letters which had to be issued to give instructions to borough officials for dealing with particular ships. Such letters, usually dealing with exemptions from the general orders for foreign ships, fishing vessels, small vessels, or particular vessels, give detailed information about the burdensome task imposed upon borough officials, who had the job of applying a general administrative order to particular cases.[112] Vessels listed by name in various letters were exempted by orders allowing them to go freely after the bailiffs of the ports had taken security from the shipmasters that they would not divert their courses to leave England or, in another case, that they would not harm the king if released.[113] The handling of such security must have involved safe custody of the property given as security and accurate records in order that masters returning with proper receipts could reclaim their security. Such general orders for impressment of merchant vessels were clearly in effect in 1215, 1223, 1224, 1229, 1230, 1235, 1242, 1253-54, and 1297.[114]

In view of the methods used in collecting royal fleets, the introductory words of a letter patent in 1226 seem ironic rather than convincing: "The king, to his proved men of Yarmouth, Dunwich, Ipswich, Oreford, and all his other faithful men who have come to Portsmouth for going into his service, greeting. Because you have come willingly to Portsmouth for going into

---

111. *Rot. Litt. Cl.*, I, 631b; II, 19a.
112. Examples of such letters are *ibid.*, I, 559a-b, 600b; *C.R. 1227-31*, pp. 206, 255, 258.
113. *Rot. Litt. Cl.*, I, 579a, 602b.
114. *Rot. Litt. Cl.*, I, 197a, 569b; *Pat. R., I,* 483; II, 259, 264; *C.R. 1234-37,* p. 161; *C.R. 1237-42,* p. 431; *C.R. 1251-53,* pp. 456, 481; *C.R. 1253-54,* pp. 26, 58, 118; *C.C.R. 1296-1302,* p. 76.

our service, we give you many thanks." In this case, the "voluntary" efforts of the men who had brought their ships were in
vain, for the decision had been made to disband the fleet, and
the vessels were granted license to return to their home ports
with the king's assurance that their trouble in assembling was
worthy of remuneration.[115]

Because of their position in naval affairs, the men in the
English ports were given various supplemental orders. Some
of these references deal with sending sailors rather than ships
into royal service. Alan Bolifrey, who was sent to London to
supervise the construction of eight transport ships in 1206, received his wages from the Londoners, and the burgesses of Ipswich made payments to forty-eight sailors and two shipmasters for nine days that same year.[116] The bailiffs of Southampton and of Portsmouth were ordered to choose thirty
sailors from the men in their boroughs who were qualified to
serve the king in his large ships, and the Cinque Ports were
required to provide one hundred and eighty good sailors to
man royal galleys and one ship.[117] Sailors for the king's ships
and galleys were obtained from the Cinque Ports in 1229 and
1244.[118] With respect to the king's galleys, the burgesses at
several ports were assigned responsibilities including service
in the galleys, repair, equipping, and custody of galleys at
Bristol, Ipswich, Dunwich, Portsmouth, and Winchelsea.[119]
In the case of a stolen ship, justice was done by ordering
bailiffs of the ports to seize the vessel until the rightful owners
could claim it.[120] In 1241 the king ordered the officials of all
ports to be on the lookout for a ship reported to be sailing

115. *Pat. R.*, I, 444; II, 44.
116. *P.R. 8 John*, pp. xvj-xvij, 55; *P.R. 9 John*, pp. 167-168.
117. *Pat. R.*, II, 34, 36; *Rot. Litt. Cl.*, II, 113a.
118. *Pat. R.*, II, 276; *C.R. 1242-47*, p. 245.
119. *Rot. Litt. Pat.*, pp. 52a, 61b, 80a; *Rot. Litt. Cl.*, I, 29a; *C.R. 1227-31*, pp.
180, 311; *C.R. 1231-34*, pp. 26, 28; *C.P.R. 1232-47*, p. 27; *C.P.R. 1258-66*, p. 152;
C.L.R., II, 78, 84, 108; *C.R. 1242-47*, p. 197.
120. *Pat. R.*, II, 144; *C.R. 1234-37*, p. 253.

around the English coast while investigating the state of the realm, to seize this ship if it put into their port for supplies, and to notify the king at once of any action taken.[121]

The many activities of local officials in the ports amounted to a general regulation of sailing in accordance with numerous writs relaying the royal military and naval policy at a particular time. For example, general prohibition of all ships leaving English ports, unless by special license of the king, is evident in 1205, 1213, 1215, and 1225.[122] A rather broader policy was laid down in 1221 for the men of the Cinque Ports, calling upon them to guard the coast diligently and to permit no knight, serjeant, or anyone else, whether armed or not, who might bring harm to the kingdom to leave or enter their ports except by special order of the king or his justices.[123] For more efficient control of cross-Channel traffic, the king issued an order to the Cinque Ports in 1226 that no one, either foot soldier or horseman, should cross the Channel from any port except Dover without special orders from the king.[124] Later in the year the officials at a number of ports were commanded to allow no one to leave with the intention of sailing to any place within the power of the French king.[125] During the frequent periods of warfare, local officials were expected to enforce a prohibition upon the export of valuable horses fit for military use.[126]

When a truce with the king of France was about to come to an end in 1229, Henry III sent a letter to many English ports announcing this fact and warning them that French ships were preparing to seize English trading vessels along the coasts of the Continent. To prevent English ships from falling into French hands, he ordered the officials of English ports not to

121. *C.R. 1237-42*, p. 352.
122. *Rot. Litt. Pat.*, p. 50a; *Rot. Litt. Cl.*, I, 133a, 198a; II, 55b.
123. *Pat. R.*, I, 284.
124. *Ibid.*, II, 25.
125. *Rot. Litt. Cl.*, II, 146a.
126. *C.R. 1227-31*, pp. 95, 197; *C.R. 1237-42*, pp. 83, 170.

allow any ships to leave after the expiration of the truce until further orders from the king.[127] The control of sailing was exercised by port officials over entry to England in 1231 when they received orders not to permit the entry of anyone from lands under French control or the entry of Richard Marsh and his supporters.[128] The following year a mandate was sent to the bailiffs of several ports not to allow any soldier, serjeant, or crossbowman from overseas to proceed inland from their ports.[129] In 1233 the Cinque Ports and Portsmouth were ordered to prevent two supporters of Richard Marsh from proceeding overseas.[130]

Other royal letters ordering borough officials to apply strict control over various persons wishing to enter or leave England were issued throughout the thirteenth century. The king received a report in 1237 that knights and serjeants from Flanders were coming to England in the guise of merchants and plotting to disturb the border area near Scotland. He immediately ordered the bailiffs of Northampton, York, Carlisle, Newcastle-on-Tyne, Nottingham, and Lancaster to arrest any military man found entering the country from Flanders.[131] The barons and bailiffs of Dover were ordered to halt any cleric planning to cross the Channel unless he was willing to take an oath not to interfere with certain projects of the king.[132] In 1258 the barons of the Cinque Ports were ordered to prevent the entry of the bishop of St. Andrews in Scotland, because he had obtained papal grants in Rome directed against King Alexander of Scotland, son-in-law of Henry III.[133] Because the king wished in 1282 to keep the tenth granted by the clergy within the country, he issued an order to the mayor and sheriffs of London to announce this policy and to arrest anyone who tried

127. *C.R. 1227-31*, p. 245.
129. *C.R. 1231-34*, p. 139.
131. *C.R. 1234-37*, p. 529.
133. *C.P.R. 1258-66*, p. 8.

128. *Ibid.*, p. 582.
130. *Ibid.*, p. 315.
132. *C.R. 1254-56*, p. 345.

to take this money out of the realm.[134] When Edward I expelled the Jews from England in 1290, he sent letters to the Cinque Ports commanding the men of the Ports to give Jews and their goods safe passage when they applied for it, and forbidding them to charge wealthy Jews exorbitant rates which would result in delaying their departure.[135] A letter of 1297 contained the order to let no one go out of the realm without a royal license and to search for letters being taken from the country; in 1298 the king ordered that no Cistercians should be allowed to leave the realm.[136]

With the extension of naval duties to a general control over shipping and transit of persons through English ports there arises the possibility of using such control for other than military purposes. Often these purposes were economic in nature (as illustrated by the order concerning a clerical tenth just mentioned), and it is apparent that officials in the ports could be used in regulating imports and exports of any goods, not just military items such as horses or grain to supply an army. Such use of the officials and men in the ports was, in fact, only one of the important ways in which burgesses served the royal administration for the regulation of commerce.

134. *C.C.R. 1279-88*, p. 157.
135. Rymer, *Foedera*, I, Pt. 2, p. 736.
136. *C.C.R. 1296-1302*, pp. 81-83, 215-216.

CHAPTER VI. THE REGULATION OF COMMERCE

NO sharp line can be drawn between control of shipping by officials in the ports for military reasons and the regulation of commerce by these officials for other reasons. In fact, the responsibilities of the officials in the latter case were also determined to a considerable extent by the military and diplomatic policies of the kings, which required not only preventing dangerous persons from entering the realm or prohibiting export of items of strategic military value, but also control over commerce dealing with commodities of indirect military value. Nor was the regulation of commerce limited solely to times of war. Peacetime regulation also is closely related to the growth of customs regulations already discussed among the financial responsibilities of the borough in Chapter III. In addition to being used to regulate maritime commerce, burgesses in all the boroughs were pressed into service for enforcement of royal regulations on domestic trade, and toward the end of the thirteenth century some of these responsibilities were becoming matters of statutory law. The legal statement often made explicit what had already come to be the practice, illustrating an attitude toward law that saw in a statute the consolidation of previous experience rather than a field for innovation.

Whatever the reasons for royal mandates to boroughs on maritime commerce, the task of the borough officials in executing them was the same—either to prohibit the export of certain goods, or to seize certain goods coming into their ports. Because many of the leading English boroughs of the early thirteenth century were also ports, responsibility for the regulation of maritime commerce and the practical application of royal directives on the subject rested with many borough officials throughout England. The military aspects of some orders to regulate commerce are expressed in mandates to the boroughs. For example, in 1216 John ordered the bailiffs of Dunwich to take security from the masters of several ships in this port to insure that cargoes of wine and other merchandise would be delivered to York or to some other town in the kingdom and not diverted "into Scotland or elsewhere in the lands of the king's enemies."[1] That same year the king ordered the mayor of Lynn and bailiffs of the count of Arundel to allow other English ships to return to their home ports with cargoes of foodstuffs, provided that security had been taken for all the ships to insure they would not be diverted to the king's enemies.[2]

Most common among the commodities prohibited from being exported was grain, and at least some of the orders regarding grain had a military purpose, even though not expressed in the writs themselves, for a large supply was necessary in the preparation of any important expedition. A general order prohibiting the export of grain was issued on April 13, 1225, and repeated in October, with copies sent to bailiffs of

1. *Rot. Litt. Cl.,* I, 260a.
2. *Ibid.,* p. 256a.

many English ports. They were to prohibit any grain from leaving their port for markets overseas under penalty of having their goods and chattels seized for the king, and to enforce this policy they were authorized to arrest persons planning to export grain and to seize sailors and cargoes aboard ships until the king should order otherwise.[3] The enforcement of similar royal prohibitions on grain and foodstuffs continued at various times throughout the thirteenth century.

Early in the reign of Edward I a new commodity was made subject to such a policy when the export of wool was banned in an effort to bring economic pressure to bear upon the countess of Flanders because of an unsettled dispute between the two rulers.[4] In one case arising from this ban, the bailiffs of Yarmouth were directed to return nine sacks of wool to a London merchant when the owner successfully appealed to the king against the confiscation, on the grounds that he had transported the wool toward the sea more than a month before hearing of the royal prohibition, and that he had previously obtained a license for the export of those nine sacks.[5]

The enforcement of such a general prohibition and the burden it meant for officials in the ports can best be traced among the letters granting exemptions from the general order sent out from the chancery to particular ports. All the ports probably received such letters at some time during the period of enforcement; a few may be cited as examples. The usual letter of this type follows the pattern of a letter close to the bailiffs of Ipswich in 1225 after the general order forbidding the export of grain issued earlier in the year. It opens with the following sentence: "We command you, notwithstanding (*non obstante*) our order that we gave for you not to permit grain to be shipped from your port to territories overseas, that you

3. *Ibid.*, II, 72a, 82b.   4. *C.P.R. 1272-81*, p. 48.
5. *C.C.R. 1272-79*, p. 86.

permit two boats . . . loaded with grain to leave for Winchelsea freely and without impediment. . . ." However, the bailiffs were required to take security to insure that the grain was not diverted to other markets, and the owners of the ships had to obtain letters patent from the bailiffs of the ports where they discharged their cargoes testifying to the fact that they had indeed brought the cargo to the authorized destination.[6] Apparently, borough officials were allowed no discretion in the enforcement of a general prohibition of exports and could allow exemptions only to those who had obtained letters from the king. In 1225 even ship owners from the Cinque Ports and other English ports were required to give security or hostages in pledging that they would transport cargoes of grain only to their own ports, and to obtain letters patent from the bailiffs of their home ports to prove that the grain actually stayed in England.[7]

Another kind of commercial regulation was that resulting from royal mandates directed against foreign merchants in general and against merchants from particular countries. These orders, proclaimed throughout the thirteenth century, supported military or political objectives of the English king and were also used as a means of forcing foreign rulers to give protection to English merchants in their lands. The policy of arresting foreign merchants from a country entering a war against England was stated in Magna Carta as follows:

And if such persons are found in our land at the beginning of a war, they shall be arrested without injury to their bodies or goods until we or our chief justice can ascertain how the merchants of our land who may then be found in the land at war with us are to be treated. And if our men are to be safe, the others shall be safe in our land.[8]

Another reason for arresting foreign merchants was based upon

6. *Rot. Litt. Cl.*, II, 87b.   7. *Ibid.*, p. 34b.
8. Stubbs, *Select Charters*, p. 298.

a system of vicarious liability that had developed in mercantile practices between towns.[9] For example, ill treatment of a London merchant in Bordeaux might result in reprisal by the Londoners against the first ship from Bordeaux to land in London, irrespective of whether the owner of the ship had any personal connection with the treatment accorded the Londoner. Sometimes such an injured English merchant appealed to the king himself and obtained royal orders directed to officials in the English ports ordering seizure of goods up to the amount of his loss from any ships entering England from the foreign port where the loss had been sustained.

In view of the generally unfriendly relations between the kings of France and England in the early thirteenth century, it is not surprising that the most frequent references to seizure of merchandise and other stringent restrictions on commerce were concerned with the merchants of France. In 1216 the bailiffs of Yarmouth were commanded to allow ships loaded with merchandise from many other places to go freely, but to seize the ships from France and Picardy.[10] Orders for seizure of French merchants and their goods were also dispatched in 1224, 1225, 1226, 1235, and 1242.[11] For example, in 1226 letters were sent to all the sheriffs and the bailiffs of several leading boroughs with orders to have proclaimed in their districts that all merchants, knights, and other persons of the power of France were free to leave England with their goods prior to a certain date, and that if they later came to England in defiance of the king's prohibition, they and their goods would be seized. In furtherance of this policy, two months later letters were issued ordering borough officials to seize any French merchants

9. For a discussion of this principle, see Erwin F. Meyer, "Some Aspects of *Withernam* or the English Mediaeval System of Vicarious Liability," *Speculum*, VIII (1933), p. 237.

10. *Rot. Litt. Cl.*, I, 642b.

11. *Ibid.*, I, 632b, 655a; II, 25a, 38a, 41a, 155b; *C.R. 1231-34*, p. 455; *C.R. 1234-37*, pp. 24, 54, 89, 90; *C.R. 1237-42*, p. 472.

and their goods and to send lists of these goods to the king.[12] In 1299 officials of many boroughs received orders to make an inquiry about goods seized by Englishmen and Gascons from Frenchmen before the late war and not since consumed, because the Pope had specified in his arbitration award that mutual restitution of such goods should be made.[13]

The responsibilities of borough officials were increased by exemptions granted to certain French merchants, and a change of policy in 1226 allowing French ships loaded with grain or foodstuffs to come freely to England except for the usual customs and debts owed to men in England.[14] Sometimes mistakes were made by officials who arrested merchants as French from areas not under control of the king of France; merchants from Boulogne, Gascony, Anjou, Bayonne, and Bruges were arrested on various occasions in the belief they were carrying goods from areas under French control.[15]

At various times a general policy directed against all foreign merchants was proclaimed with a flurry of chancery activity attempting to translate the broad policy into specific action by local officials. The course of one such venture is seen in a series of letters in 1229. First, on July 5 the sheriffs throughout England and the bailiffs of fifteen leading English boroughs were sent letters close ordering them to proclaim that no foreign merchant from any land should remain with their goods and chattels in England after a certain date. English officials were ordered to seize alien merchants and their goods remaining in England after the specified time. On July 20 the bailiffs of several ports were ordered not to allow any foreign merchants from lands not under the power of the English king to cross the Channel before the specified date without a special

12. *Rot. Litt. Cl.*, II, 155b, 159a.
13. *C.P.R. 1292-1301*, p. 438.
14. Examples of exemptions may be found in *Rot. Litt. Cl.*, I, 603a; II, 5b, 25a and the policy change in II, 205b.
15. *Ibid.*, II, 7b, 87b; *C.R. 1227-31*, pp. 204, 278.

order of the king, and to arrest foreign merchants after that date as previously ordered. A further letter of July 25 ordered the mayor and sheriffs of London to allow all foreign merchants, except those from lands under the power of the French king, to remain in England after the term set for their departure, notwithstanding the previous order.[16]

Merchants from small, politically weak lands were often caught up in such sweeping bans, along with the subjects of the more powerful French king. Mercantile disputes of a localized nature accounted for the arrest of other merchants with whose ruler the English king had no quarrel; but whether the arrest involved a grandiose display of royal policy or a petty merchants' quarrel, the enforcement of the royal will depended upon the co-operation of officials in the ports, as well as the sheriffs and other royal officials. Selected from among merchants arrested at various times in English ports are men from the land of the Count of St. Giles, St. Omer, Douai, the land of the Duke of Louvain, lands north of the Alps, Ghent, Scotland, Bordeaux, St. Valery and Barbeflete, Holland and Zeeland, Brabant, Gascony, and Lombardy.[17]

In an unusual and not altogether creditable use of royal power Henry III commanded the mayor of London in 1245 to convoke all the merchants from north of the Alps who engaged in money-changing and to tell them on his behalf that they were to provide him with a considerable sum of money in return for the privilege they enjoyed in making profits from money-changing, or else leave the country within a certain

16. *C.R. 1227-31*, pp. 244-246.
17. *Rot. Litt. Cl.*, I, 145a, 612b; II, 136a; *Rot. Litt. Pat.*, p. 105a; *C.R. 1227-31*, pp. 49, 55; *C.R. 1231-34*, p. 58; *C.R. 1237-42*, p. 239; *C.R. 1254-56*, p. 384; *C.R. 1259-61*, p. 489; *C.R. 1264-68*, p. 64; *C.P.R. 1266-72*, p. 386; *C.C.R. 1288-96*, p. 300; *C.C.R. 1302-07*, pp. 4, 6, 110; *Curia Regis Rolls*, XII, 455; Thomas, *Calendar of Early Mayor's Court Rolls*, p. 21. See also Jean de Sturler, *Les relations politiques et les échanges commerciaux entre le duché de Brabant et l'Angleterre au moyen âge* (Paris, 1936), pp. 99-102.

period.[18] In 1251 the king acted against Italian money men when the sheriffs of London were ordered to arrest all merchants from Florence and Siena for usury, and similarly in 1274 London officials were ordered to proclaim that all merchant usurers must leave England within twenty days or face arrest.[19]

Flemish merchants were frequently singled out for restrictive action in disputes between the English king and the ruler in Flanders and in retribution for treatment of English merchants.[20] Difficulties in executing the royal will in one such case can be followed in the records of London giving the return of the citizens to the king's writ. Because of the seizure near Sandwich of two ships from Genoa by Flemish malefactors and the failure of the Flemish ruler to make restoration, the king ordered that Flemish goods be seized to the value of 522 marks. London officials seized about 520 marks of goods, but the citizens of London from whom cloth to the value of three hundred marks had been taken claimed the cloth was their own at the time of seizure and offered to prove this. However, the mayor and sheriffs thought that the offer had been made in bad faith and postponed further proceedings until receiving further orders from the king. Royal letters on the subject continued to be issued into January of 1304.[21]

Another good example of the burden placed upon borough officials in carrying out royal orders in regard to commercial regulation is found in a rather involved case from 1295. The king received a complaint from English merchants that they had been robbed by Spanish mariners when they were in the dominion of the king of Portugal. In order to verify this com-

18. C.R. 1242-47, pp. 317-318.
19. C.R. 1251-53, p. 3; C.C.R. 1272-79, p. 108.
20. Rot. Litt. Pat., p. 85b; Rot. Litt. Cl., I, 210b, 211a; C.R. 1231-34, pp. 13, 14, 18; Cronica Maiorum et Vicecomitum, pp. 126-127, 135-137, 138, 140; C.P.R. 1266-72, pp. 469, 587; C.R. 1268-72, p. 331; C.P.R 1272-81, p. 95.
21. Sharpe, Calendar of Letter-Books. Letter-Book C, pp. 123-124; C.P.R. 1301-07, pp. 158, 210; C.C.R. 1302-07, pp. 50, 55, 56.

plaint, the king appointed a clerk, the mayor and bailiff of Southampton, the bailiffs of Portsmouth, and the bailiffs of Winchelsea to hold inquisitions among the men of their towns. All Spanish goods found were to be seized, appraised, and given into the custody of townsmen chosen in each port for this job. The confiscated goods were then to be delivered to the injured English merchants in proportion to their losses, but they were required to give security in case other merchants might also have claims against the Spanish. Nothing was done about carrying out the original order, so a second mandate had to be sent from the chancery to make sure that something was done.[22]

In addition to this control over maritime commerce, the responsibilities of the borough extended to the market place, where the variety of tasks imposed is more significant of the usefulness of the boroughs than the small number of such references. The mayor and reeves of Northampton were expected to aid royal officials sent in 1218 to take wool there by having the wool taken for the king immediately appraised by view and testimony of lawful men from their city. This wool was then offered for sale and if no one wished to buy it, the borough officials were asked to advise and aid in obtaining carts to transport the wool to London.[23] In 1225 the bailiffs and two burgesses of Marlborough aided the constable there in the sale of surplus grain and wine from Marlborough castle.[24] On several occasions the king's buyers got first choice in sales of falcons by having the selling delayed by borough officials until they could arrive.[25] The mayor and bailiffs of Lincoln were ordered in 1223 on behalf of the king (*ex parte nostra*) to forbid any market to be held in the cemetery in the future and to provide a more suitable place.[26] In 1235 the mayor and

22. *C.C.R. 1288-96*, pp. 408-409.   23. *Rot. Litt. Cl.*, I, 383a.
24. *Ibid.*, II, 42a.   25. *Ibid.*, I, 20a; *Pat. R.*, I, 332.
26. *Rot. Litt. Cl.*, I, 547b.

sheriffs of London were ordered to proclaim and to prohibit firmly anyone from refusing to sell to London Jews any items publicly exposed for sale.[27] In order to meet a shortage of grain in 1238, the king ordered a proclamation in Lynn that all persons having grain in storage which they planned to sell should make it available for immediate sale to rich or poor.[28]

In regard to the marketplace, the most important responsibility of borough officials was the enforcement of royal assizes of wine. A question about persons selling wine contrary to the assize was included among the articles of the general eyre, and royal letters during the thirteenth century give more specific references to enforcement of this assize within boroughs.[29] For example, a general letter to the boroughs in 1223 announced a decision by the king's council to the effect that no sester of wine should be sold for more than six pence (except in a few boroughs where the price was set at eight pence) and ordered officials of the boroughs to proclaim and enforce this assize.[30] A dispute over these responsibilities occurred in London in 1256 when the justiciar presented the mayor and sheriffs with a royal letter ordering them to bring all vintners of the city before his court at the Tower for breach of the assize. The citizens resisted on the ground that they only need answer for this offense at the court of common pleas, but the justiciar replied that seven years was too long an interval to let the vintners break the assize. The citizens answered that the king should cause an election to be held among the citizens for choosing two wardens of the assize in place of those who had died, but the whole question was finally postponed until it could be taken up by the king himself.[31] The point at issue

27. *C.R. 1234-37*, p. 329.   28. *C.R. 1237-42*, p. 133.
29. Stubbs, *Select Charters*, p. 254; *Rot. Litt. Cl.*, I, 631b; II, 149a; Maitland, *Select Pleas*, I, 98; *C.R. 1234-37*, pp. 407, 523; *C.R. 1256-59*, p. 182; *C.C.R. 1288-96*, p. 284.
30. *Rot. Litt. Cl.*, I, 568a-b.
31. *Cronica Maiorum et Vicecomitum*, pp. 25-26.

was answered when a statute in 1278 provided for annual inquiries requiring the mayor and bailiffs to present cases about breaking the assize of wine before the two barons of the exchequer who made visitations about disseisins. If the borough officials waited until the coming of the justices in eyre, they were to be amerced for their negligence.[32]

Officials in the boroughs had some responsibilties in regard to commercial debts early in the thirteenth century, and other responsibilities were assigned them by statute toward the end of the century. Seizure of goods as distraints for debts were carried out by borough officials on royal orders at various times.[33] Somewhat similar was the action taken in 1304 when the king ordered the sheriffs of London to attach all members of a certain Florentine society in order that they would have to appear before the king and his council. Such measures were necessary because it was feared the members of the London branch were preparing to leave the country without paying their obligations, just as the branch at Paris had already done.[34] That same year the sheriffs were ordered to prohibit the further alienation of letters of obligation drawn against the king for wages paid a knight but assigned to certain merchants for provisions before the date payable.[35]

The defiinite procedure established for the recognizance of debts by the Statute of Merchants (also called the Statute of Acton Burnel) enacted in 1283 drew the officials of a few leading boroughs into the enforcement machinery. A merchant should cause his debtor to come before the mayor of London, York, Lincoln, Winchester, Shrewsbury, or Bristol and a clerk appointed by the king, where the debtor would acknowledge his debt. The clerk entered the recognizance on a roll and drew

32. *Statutes of the Realm*, I, 50.
33. *C.R. 1227-31*, pp. 136, 142, 383, 561; *C.R. 1237-42*, p. 370; *C.R. 1247-51*, p. 552.
34. *C.C.R. 1302-07*, p. 175.
35. *Ibid.*, p. 187.

up a bill obligatory which the mayor and clerk sealed with a special royal seal in their custody for this purpose. If the debt were unpaid when due, the creditor could reappear before the same officials, and the mayor would cause the movables, chattels, and devisable burgages of the debtor to be sold in amount of the debt as established by the appraisal of honest men. If there were no buyer, the property was turned over to the creditor by the mayor. If the debtor had no movables in the jurisdiction of the mayor, he should send the recognizance made before him and the clerk to the chancellor, and the chancellor would order the appropriate sheriff to execute the same procedure. Two years later, some changes were made providing that the roll of debts be made in duplicate, with the mayor or chief warden of a town keeping one copy and the clerk the other; also, the seal was to be in two pieces, with the mayor keeping the larger and the clerk the smaller piece. Enforcement was simply by arrest of the debtor with no provision retained for sale of his goods.[36]

A similar procedure for acknowledgment of debt had been followed at the Guildhall with recognizances entered in municipal records as early as 1275, and when the statute was passed, the mayor, sheriffs, and leading men of London met and decided that the chamberlain of London should continue to receive recognizances of debts, notwithstanding the statute. A long list of recognizances that continued to be made at the Guildhall follows in the record.[37] Royal letters to Winchester in 1302 contained orders for the transfer of the seal used in making recognizances of debts and for action by the mayor in conjunction with a royal clerk in enforcing the statute.[38] In 1300 the mayor and sheriffs of London were ordered to release a man imprisoned in Newgate for debt because the man was a

36. *Statutes of the Realm*, I, 53-54, 99.
37. Sharpe, *Calendar of Letter-Books. Letter-Book A*. pp. 3, 79.
38. *C.P.R. 1301-07*, p. 9; *C.C.R. 1296-1302*, p. 512.

clerk.[39] In 1302 the mayor and another man in London were taking recognizances of debts, and the mayor and sheriffs had also imprisoned a man in Newgate by virtue of the statute.[40]

From international relations to the debts of individuals royal policy affected the boroughs, and these policies, in turn, were made effective throughout England only by use of burgesses in administering them. Because the trade and commerce of the nation centered in the boroughs, use of burgesses in this field was quite natural, but it was also part of the general pattern by which an expanding central administration communicated its control to the local level. Once the precedent of giving administrative responsibilities to the burgesses was established, it was capable of considerable expansion.

39. *C.C.R. 1296-1302*, p. 333.
40. *Ibid.*, pp. 520-521.

CHAPTER VII. OTHER ADMINISTRA-
TIVE RESPONSIBILITIES

A MONG the most important administrative responsibilties
of the boroughs in addition to those discussed in the previous chapters were ones that could be classified under the
heading of special services. These services which the burgesses
provided for the king included transportation of men and
materials, purveyance of food and supplies, and the construction and maintenance of royal buildings and equipment. Purveyance alone accounted for more administrative activity on the
part of officials in the boroughs than almost any other activity
they were called upon to perform for the king. Additional
responsibilities were the administering of royal property or
revenue, enforcement of protection for the Jews, proclaiming
royal policy and commands, and giving counsel and advice
to the king and his council.

Of the transportation services, one of the most frequently
used was the providing of ships for crossing the Channel to
the Continent. In the later twelfth century, each time the
king or some of his immediate family crossed, the expense
appeared on the pipe roll as an allowance to some local adminis-

trative unit, often a borough.[1] Allowances were made at other times for the passage of prominent ecclesiastics, the king's constable, foreign dignitaries, men going into royal service, messengers, and other prominent men on royal business or enjoying the king's favor.[2]

Such allowances for passage appeared frequently on the account for Southampton, which seems to have been the usual port for embarkation and where the king's galley was ordinarily kept. Early in the thirteenth century Dover came to be the usual point of departure and continued to be so throughout the century, but most records for Dover, other than those that associate the "mayor" or the "barons" with the bailiffs, do not serve as indications of activity by burgesses because the bailiffs there were royal appointees. In addition, Portsmouth was important in this cross-Channel ferrying, and the following boroughs also received orders to provide transportation either across the Channel or from England to Ireland: Bristol, Dunwich, Ipswich, Portsmouth, Sandwich, and Yarmouth.[3]

When the royal court traveled about the country during this period, another important responsibility for the boroughs was to provide for the transportation of supplies and equipment needed by the court and by the governmental departments and justices in carrying out their official duties. For such services the boroughs were usually compensated by an allowance from their farm at the exchequer, but the compensation could take some other form. Many of the orders for transportation are found in connection with purveyance, and, therefore, it is not surprising to find that the important centers for purveyance,

---

1. *P.R. 22 Hen. II*, p. 199. See also the discussion of the king's galley in *P.R. 33 Hen. II*, p. xxi.
2. *P.R. 22 Hen. II*, p. 200; *P.R. 24 Hen. II*, pp. 112-113; *P.R. 4 Ric. I*, p. 308; *Rotuli de Liberate*, p. 84; *Rot. Litt. Cl.*, I, 22b, 81b, 104b, 207a, 208b, 229a, 548b, 557b, 599a; II, 168a.
3. *C.L.R.*, II, 172; *C.R. 1227-31*, p. 298; *C.R. 1231-34*, p. 404; *C.R. 1254-56*, p. 95; *C.R. 1256-59*, pp. 58, 302; *C.R. 1261-64*, p. 393; *C.C.R. 1296-1302*, p. 349.

London and Southampton, are also outstanding in the number of entries for transportation services.

Transportation entries for London illustrate the variety of items transported: equipment of the king and household, rolls of the exchequer and the exchequer of the Jews, the king's treasure, wine, meat, money, foodstuffs, robes, spices, and wood for gallows.[4] Transportation entries after 1240 seem to show that writs of *computate* and *allocate* (which provide the best source for this subject) were ordinarily enrolled on the *liberate* rolls rather than the close rolls; an entry in the close roll of 1240 was canceled because that same entry was in the *liberate* rolls.[5] During the period 1240 to 1260 when such entries are found mainly in the published *liberate* rolls, London received an average of one order for transportation every two months.[6] However, an example of a similar entry in connection with the transportation of the royal treasure takes the form of a letter patent issued on August 18, 1242, to all sheriffs, reeves of towns, and other bailiffs through whose bailiwicks the sheriffs of London would pass while conducting the treasure, ordering them to give aid as directed by the sheriffs to insure that the treasure would be kept safely at night and brought safely to Winchester.[7]

Borough officials at Southampton performed outstanding service in transporting wine for the royal administration because their borough was the most important center for the importation of this commodity. One long Southampton account in the pipe roll for 1230 is concerned almost exclusively with transportation of wine to various places in England, and

4. P.R. *5 John*, p. 9; P.R. *11 John*, p. 27; P.R. *3 Ric. I*, p. 136; P.R. *14 Hen. III*, p. 97; Cannon, *Pipe Roll 26 Hen. III*, p. 282; *Rot. Litt. Cl.*, I, 139b, 145b, 350b, 352b, 358a, 362a, 364a, 392a, 456a, 548a, 587a, 606a, 616b; II, 101b; C.L.R., I, 12.

5. C.R. *1237-42* p. 252.

6. An example for the year 1246 may be found in C.L.R., III, 18, 19, 39, 45, 57, 86, 95, 99.

7. C.P.R. *1232-47*, p. 301.

a second entry twelve years later is nearly as long.[8] Many transportation orders in the close rolls deal with wine, but there is considerable variety among them. Some give detailed instructions for the distribution of the wine to various places, while others specify that the shipment be sent to one place; some shipments consisted of only five tuns, but others amounted to three hundred tuns.[9]

In general, Southampton was second only to London in the number of orders for transportation, and these orders included other commodities as well as wine, even though that commodity accounted for most of the orders.[10] Other boroughs that received orders for transportation were Bridgnorth, Bristol, Cambridge, Canterbury, Colchester, Gloucester, Hereford, Kingston, Lincoln, Lynn, Newcastle-on-Tyne, Northampton, Oxford, Portsmouth, Shrewsbury, Winchelsea, Winchester, Worcester, Yarmouth, and York.[11]

Only rarely do the records give any indication of the difficulties encountered by burgesses in carrying out the king's commands to provide transportation, and therefore the few examples that do occur take on added value. Among the pleas taken before the warden and aldermen of London July 25, 1291, was a case involving John Hurel, who had been arrested and imprisoned to answer the charge of obstructing and assaulting a sheriff. The sheriffs' men had been sent to requisition carts for the purpose of moving the king's wardrobe, and although he denied using force, Hurel admitted that he did not allow those men to enter his house to make a distress because he had

8. *P.R. 14 Hen. III*, pp. 201-202; Cannon, *Pipe Roll 26 Hen. III*, p. 274. See also *P.R. 30 Hen. II*, p. xxvi.

9. *Rot. Litt. Cl.*, I, 17b, 86b, 98b, 481a, 484b.

10. *P.R. 24 Hen. II*, p. 113; *P.R. 34 Hen. II*, p. 180; *P.R. 1 Ric. I*, p. 206; Cannon, *Pipe Roll 26 Hen. III*, p. 263.

11. *P.R. 11 Hen. II*, p. 14; *P.R. 27 Hen. II*, p. 17; Hodgson, *History of Northumberland*, Pt. 3, Vol. III, col. 238; *C.L.R.*, II, 66; III, 1, 101, 104, 207, 278; IV, 401; *C.R. 1231-34*, pp. 81, 211, 267; *C.R. 1237-42*, p. 128; *C.R. 1251-53*, pp. 508-509; *C.R. 1254-56*, pp. 17, 256; *C.R. 1259-61*, p. 436; *C.R. 1261-64*, p. 32.

made no trespass. Because he confessed not allowing a sheriff to enter his house to make a distress, it was decided that he was in contempt of the king and should be imprisoned, but the coroner was told to summon twelve men for establishing all the facts in the case.[12]

Three letters to Southampton also give some insight into the problems and responsibilties of executing a royal command. In 1246 the king notified the bailiffs that he had pardoned William de Neubir' the loss of one tun of wine which he was transporting from Southampton when it was broken by misadventure on his cart, and the king, therefore, ordered the borough officials to permit William to have peace in the matter. In the same year, John Sweyn petitioned the king for quittance when a tun of wine that the bailiffs of Southampton had brought for him to carry to Reading was broken by chance on his cart before leaving the borough. The bailiffs had retained his horses for this loss, but the king ordered them to restore the horses if the facts were as Sweyn had presented.[13] In 1243 a writ was issued in favor of Walter le Flemeng, bailiff of Southampton, who was coming to render his account at the exchequer when he received a royal order to proceed to Portsmouth and prepare for shipping the king's treasure overseas. The barons of the exchequer were ordered to assign him another day to make his account.[14]

Valuable as were the transportation services provided by burgesses, the most important of the special services performed for the king was that of purveyance, obtaining of food and other supplies to satisfy his needs and desires. As used in this context, the term does not mean that the boroughs were put to great expense in providing these supplies, for nearly all the writs specifically promise that allowances will be made at the

12. Sharpe, *Calendar of Letter-Books. Letter-Book A.* p. 192.
13. *C.R. 1237-42*, pp. 216, 247.
14. *C.R. 1242-47*, p. 102.

exchequer to cover the cost of purveyance. Still, purveyance was an important service because the responsibility for obtaining the commodities rested entirely with borough officials, and because the method of payment by allowances at the exchequer made it possible for the king to manage without having to make direct money payments to meet his expenses.

The enormous variety of items supplied by the boroughs under orders from the king gives one an idea of the broad scope of borough responsibility in the matter of purveyance. The greatest number of entries are orders to provide wine, but the entries concerned with cloth and clothing are nearly as numerous. Many entries deal with harness and equipment to be provided for pack horses and saddle horses; others required the burgesses to provide horses, carts and wagons, or ships at the king's command. Wax was an important item which the burgesses were often asked to obtain for the royal household, as attested by a large number of entries scattered throughout the rolls. Entries requiring the purveyance of food sometimes were written in general terms, and at other times specific items were required, such as spices of various kinds, fish and other seafood, cheese, nuts, grain, and meat. Various kinds of hardware items and building supplies were obtained by boroughs for the royal administration. Finally, certain broad entries simply required that the burgesses provide for the necessities of some person or group.

Although the initial step in purveyance by the boroughs was a royal letter, the immediate object of such purveyance was not always the fulfilment of the king's own needs. Some items were ordered for the use of the queen, and others were purveyed for various royal relatives; even the former wife of King John was provided for in this way.[15] Other individuals not connected with the royal family sometimes benefited by re-

15. P.R. 9 John, p. 144.

ceiving items obtained by burgesses to provide a gift from the king. Another entry gave as the reason for the king's command for purveyance the repayment of a debt owed an individual. Provision of clothing and other gifts to messengers of the pope and of the Norwegian king are also listed. Finally, a large number of entries deal with purveyance for the king and his officials, either for their own use or to be used by them in the king's interest. Clerks of the household departments— the chapel, the butlery, the kitchen—are all described as receiving supplies obtained by purveyance in the boroughs.

London was the leading city for royal purveyance, and the citizens through letters to their mayor and sheriffs were required at one time or another to provide almost all the articles required from any borough. The Londoners were particularly called upon to furnish supplies for the various household departments.[16] Articles obtained were designated for use by many different persons: harness for carrying the queen's belongings, items required for the king's use, necessities for an Easter feast to be delivered to royal servants, cloth for a messenger from the king of Norway, livery provided for two of the king's falconers, clothing for the king's cousin Eleanor, robes for papal nuncios, robes for several men coming to the court from continental boroughs, and grain made into bread and pottage for daily distribution to three hundred paupers.[17] London records also make it possible to follow in detail the execution of one order for purveyance, although it involves a rather unusual item. A letter dated April 18, 1298, and addressed to the chamberlains of the city ordered that a beam for weighing wool at Lynn be made and delivered at the exchequer, but the chamberlain refused to do anything about

16. *P.R. 3 Ric. I*, p. 136; *P.R. 5 Ric. I*, p. 158; *P.R. 14 Hen. III*, p. 98; *Rotuli de Liberate*, p. 89; *Rot. Litt. Cl.*, I, 17b, 27a, 81b, 174b, 388a; II, 117a.

17. *Rotuli de Liberate*, pp. 79, 95; *Rot. Litt. Cl.*, I, 55a, 194a, 382a, 410a, 523a, 573a; II, 21a. Providing for the king's alms was a usual request to boroughs as exemplified in *C.L.R.*, IV, 1, 8, 10, 14, 25, 26, 32, 76, 90.

it until the mayor returned to the city. When he returned, another writ addressed to the mayor and chamberlain was read in London on Tuesday, and the mayor immediately ordered six woolsmen and Thomas Torgod, "scale maker," to approve the weighing beam before the city's mark was added to it. On Wednesday the mayor and citizens brought the beam to the exchequer and it was delivered to the men of Lynn.[18]

Southampton was second to London in commercial activity during the early thirteenth century and was, quite naturally, another important source for royal purveyance, especially for wine.[19] Entries of this kind are found in the pipe rolls of the later twelfth century and are extremely numerous in the chancery records throughout the early years of the next century, although these become somewhat more frequent after about 1220.[20] Bristol was another important source for royal purveyance in this period, as shown by the large number of entries in the records referring to this borough.[21] Among these entries are orders to provide clothing and other necessities for the king's cousin Eleanor, the sister of Arthur of Brittany, who was kept a prisoner in Bristol castle for some forty years after her brother was murdered.[22] In addition to the boroughs already mentioned, entries regarding purveyance before 1227 were collected for the following: Cambridge, Carlisle, Chester, Dunwich, Exeter, Gloucester, Kingston, Lincoln, Northampton, Oxford, Portsmouth, and Winchester, a city that might well have been important enough for separate mention.[23]

18. Sharpe, *Calendar of Letter-Books. Letter-Book B*, pp. 213-214.
19. Austin L. Poole, *From Domesday Book to Magna Carta 1087-1216* (Oxford, 1951), p. 437, notes that Southampton was second to London in commercial activity.
20. Examples may be found in *P.R. 23 Hen. II*, p. 177; *P.R. 32 Hen. II*, p. 179; *P.R. 34 Hen. II*, p. 180; *Rot. Litt. Cl.*, I, 41a, 46a, 89a, 589b, 600b, 623b; II, 97a.
21. Madox, *History of the Exchequer*, 376 n. (Memoranda Roll 32 Hen. III); *Rot. Litt. Cl.*, I, 275a, 593b, 604a, 619b, 622a-b, 645a, 647a; II, 37a, 158a.
22. *Rot. Litt. Cl.*, I, 624a, 649b. For comment on her imprisonment, see Poole, *Domesday Book to Magna Carta*, p. 382.
23. *Rotuli de Liberate*, pp. 2, 8; *Rot. Litt. Cl.*, I, 39b, 115a, 191b, 388a, 395a, 443b, 580a, 611b, 634b, 636a; II, 28b, 51a, 108b, 116b.

It is clear that purveyance remained an important responsibility of English burgesses throughout the thirteenth century, for the chancery rolls, especially the *liberate* rolls and the close rolls, show a large amount of activity in this connection. However, the practice of enrolling most entries of this type on the *liberate* rolls makes it impossible to judge the extent of borough purveyance after the last printed roll for 1260, even though the few references in the close rolls after that date show that purveyance did continue. In 1240 there were about twice as many entries on the *liberate* rolls as on the close rolls, and for this reason the sharp decrease in number of entries after 1260 is almost certainly due to the gap in the evidence caused by lack of printed *liberate* rolls, rather than a discontinuance of responsibility for this service.

When the boroughs are ranked according to the number of purveyance entries they received, London is shown to have been by far the most important source for royal purveyance throughout the thirteenth century, as it had been before 1227. During the years for which *liberate* rolls are available, London received a number of purveyance writs each year; in 1246 some seven entries regarding purveyance at London are found on the *liberate* roll and two on the close roll.[24] Southampton continued to be second and Bristol third. A large number of writs concerning purveyance had been addressed to Winchester before 1227, but this city ceased to be an important source for purveyance during the later period. Nearly all the boroughs named in entries before 1227 continued to be useful to the royal administration for this purpose, but no entries were found for Carlisle, Dunwich, and Exeter. Writs were also sent to the following boroughs that had not previously received purveyance orders: Bedford, Beverley, Canterbury, Colchester, Grimsby, Hereford, Ipswich, Leicester, Lynn, Newcastle-on-

24. *C.L.R.*, II, 28, 39, 46, 51, 53, 81, 84; *C.R. 1242-47*, pp. 400, 465.

Tyne, Norwich, Nottingham, Sandwich, Scarborough, Shrewsbury, Stamford, Worcester, Yarmouth, and York.[25]
Some of the boroughs were sources for particular commodities, but a wide variety of items continued to be obtained by
borough officials for the royal administration. Beverley, Leicester, and Lincoln were especially useful to the royal administration as sources for cloth and clothing.[26] Most of the Bristol
entries were concerned with wine. The Bristol custom concerning payments for grain, wine, meat, fish, or other things taken
as provisions for the royal castle was that payments should be
made within forty days to burgesses or merchants dwelling in
Bristol; if the owners were foreigners in the town, they should
be paid at once.[27] In 1241 the bailiffs were commanded to
provide tapers, other lights, and alms for the obsequies of the
king's cousin, Eleanor of Brittany.[28] The burgesses of Southampton continued to supply a large amount of wine for royal
use throughout the thirteenth century, and other commodities
were also provided. Until 1307 London entries are outstanding
for the great variety of things purveyed, as well as for the number of entries.

Purveyance by the king's own household officials did not
always mean that the burgesses were able to escape all responsibility in this connection. Writs of aid were often issued
on such occasions directing burgesses to help the officials being
sent to their districts for seizing or buying commodities.[29] The
aid might involve collecting the desired amounts of a commodity, appraising commodities taken by royal officials in

25. *C.P.R. 1232-47*, p. 23; *C.R. 1231-34*, pp. 82, 472; *C.R. 1234-37*, pp. 375,
521; *C.L.R.*, II, 260, 318, 319, 320; III, 45; IV, 349; *C.R. 1242-47*, p.
309; *C.R. 1247-51*, p. 130; *C.R. 1251-53*, p. 17; *C.R. 1253-54*, p. 46; *C.R.
1254-56*, p. 8; *C.R. 1259-61*, p. 245; *C.R. 1261-64*, p. 34; *C.C.R. 1288-96*, p. 407.
26. *P.R. 16 Hen. II*, p. 154; *Rot. Litt. Cl.*, II, 28b, 116b; *C.R. 1234-37*, p. 301.
27. Bateson, *Borough Customs*, II, 88.
28. *C.L.R.*, II, 68.
29. *C.P.R. 1232-47*, pp. 97, 407; *C.P.R. 1247-58*, p. 228; *C.L.R.*, IV, 115, 129,
159.

order to establish a fair value for compensation, paying the owner for the goods taken, or providing expert knowledge about the quality of certain goods to be purveyed. A prominent feature of the chancery entries concerning purveyance was certain regular purveyance exacted from some boroughs on Christmas, Easter, and other feast days. Such entries occur year after year in the rolls, and usually contain orders for purveyance of food; bread, wine, and fish are especially prominent among the particular items purveyed. Lists of places that supplied food for such feasts usually included a number of manors and a few boroughs.[30]

Some of the orders for transportation or for purveyance involved materials needed for the construction or repair of buildings or equipment. More often the burgesses did the work, and sometimes they provided money to meet the immediate costs involved. Nevertheless, it should be emphasized that the total amount of these services was never very important. Most of the scattered entries deal with castles; the burgesses were called upon to provide money to meet construction costs, to supply stone, and to make repairs upon castles and the buildings enclosed within their walls.[31]

Of the few entries that are not routine in nature, a letter of 1243 is unusual for its order that the mayor and bailiffs of Winchester were to set up certain metes and bounds from the wall of the city in order that when the moat of the castle was dug those guides would serve to keep it everywhere at least twelve feet from the wall.[32] The zeal of the men of Bristol in taking stone for the repair of a castle had to be curbed by ordering them to return the stone to the monks of

30. C.R. 1231-34, p. 172; C.R. 1234-37, p. 402; C.R. 1268-72, pp. 10-11.
31. P.R. 28 Hen. II, p. 152; P.R. 30 Hen. II, p. 150; P.R. 3 Ric. I, p. 136; P.R. 4 John, p. 78; P.R. 14 John, p. 88; P.R. 14 Hen. III, p. 1; Rot. Litt. Cl., I, 359a, 402b, 433a, 450b, 613a; II, 20a, 93a; C.R. 1227-31, p. 498; C.R. 1231-34, p. 246; C.L.R., II, 36, 146, 198; III, 313, 314; C.R. 1251-53, p. 113; C.P.R. 1281-92, p. 13.
32. C.L.R., II, 195.

St. Thomas, who had collected it for transporting to Dublin, where they intended to build a church.[33] On another occasion the mayor and bailiffs at Bristol were told to elect four men to view the works at Bristol with the provision that these men would be quit of tallage and common pleas; seven months later one of these men had to be replaced because he was frequently away from the town on business trips to Ireland.[34] When a royal license was granted to the master and brethren of the hospital at Portsmouth to enclose part of the king's highway, provided they enlarge it an equal amount on the other side, the bailiffs and good men of Portsmouth were ordered to view the work.[35]

Among the other types of construction services mentioned, a surprising number of entries deal with the construction and repair of royal jails within boroughs.[36] A Bristol entry of 1226 is somewhat unusual because a royal official, the constable of Bristol castle, was ordered to provide wood for the construction of the jail by borough officials.[37] Construction work or repair of the king's houses within a borough are mentioned a number of times, bridges were built and repaired at London, and some entries even deal with the repair of equipment.[38] The king ordered the repair of the wharves at London, and on several occasions at Southampton.[39]

The miscellaneous administrative responsibilities of the boroughs in addition to those special services discussed above include a variety of activities that could best be described as

33. *C.R. 1247-51*, p. 526.
34. *Ibid.*, p. 432; *C.R. 1251-53*, p. 178.
35. *C.P.R. 1247-58*, p. 219.
36. *P.R. 29 Hen. III*, p. 148; *P.R. 4 John*, p. 79; *P.R. 14 John*, p. 23; *Rot. Litt. Cl.*, I, 398a, 452a, 522b.
37. *Rot. Litt. Cl.*, II, 93b.
38. *P.R. 23 Hen. II*, p. 177; *P.R. 3 Ric. I*, p. 136; *P.R. 4 John*, p. 78; *P.R. 13 John*, p. 132; *P.R. 14 Hen. III*, p. 202; *Rot. Litt. Cl.*, I, 136a, 156b, 340b, 509b, 589a, 601b; II, 63a, 94a, 126a, 143b; *Rotuli de Liberate*, p. 28; *C.L.R.*, II, 5, 229; III, 13, 16, 101, 140, 154, 176, 201, 241.
39. *Rot. Litt. Cl.*, I, 174a, 484b; II, 64a.

executive or administrative functions, in the limited sense of borough officials serving as administrators of crown property or revenue. Execution of justice and custody of chattels forfeited by criminals as discussed in Chapter IV among the judicial activities of the borough exemplify but one aspect of the responsibility to serve as agents of the king in administering property or revenue and the execution or royal commands.

In the later twelfth and early thirteenth centuries borough officials sometimes managed escheats for the king.[40] A similar responsibility stated in the custumal of about 1272 at Portsmouth was for the borough officials to seize land for default of rent:

Also if it be so that ther be any lond or tenement withyn the fraunches that [is] behynd of king's rent a yer and a day, hit is lefull to all meyrs and the bayly to distresse uppon the seif lond and tenements with the king's yard, and if ther be found no distress thereon, the meyr and the bayly may lefu[lly] sease it for the king.[41]

Borough officials also administered lands for the king where there is no specific reference to escheats.[42] Certain boroughs farmed the revenues of districts not included in the borough farm and accounted for these districts at the exchequer.[43] Undoubtedly the best known farm of this type was the grant of Middlesex to "my citizens of London" by Henry I; they also accounted for the small district called Queenhithe in the late twelfth century.[44]

Burgesses were given custody of various royal property

40. *P.R. 23 Hen. II*, p. 119; *P.R. 24 Hen. II*, p. 9; *P.R. 34 Hen. II*, p. 81; *P.R. 14 Hen. III*, p. 66; *Rot. Litt. Cl.*, I, 124b.
41. Bateson, *Borough Customs*, I, 301.
42. *P.R. 21 Hen. II*, p. 157; *P.R. 14 Hen. III*, pp. 56, 58; Cannon, *Pipe Role 26 Hen. III*, p. 239; *Memoranda Roll 1230-31*, p. 66.
43. *P.R. 31 Hen. I*, p. 142; *P.R. 2 John*, p. 266; *P.R. 7 John*, pp. 128, 223; *P.R. 13 John*, pp. 44, 264; *P.R. 14 Hen. III*, pp. 224-225; Mills and Stewart-Brown, *Cheshire in the Pipe Rolls*, p. 39; Cannon, *Pipe Roll 26 Hen. III*, pp. 3, 87, 308; *B.B.C.*, I, 225; Mills, *Pipe Roll for 1295*, pp. 4, 8.
44. *B.B.C.*, I, 220; *P.R. 3 Ric. I*, p. 136.

including the royal treasure at Bristol, falcons at Lynn and Grimsby, money from a judicial eyre at Oxford, lead at Southampton, bridges and hurdles for ships at Portsmouth, grain at Scarborough, and wine at many other boroughs.[45] Several borough officials managed the sale of wine both from that in their custody and that delivered to them by royal officials.[46] In 1271 wool and fells were seized from the Flemings and placed in custody of an individual burgess at Newcastle-on-Tyne, but some twenty-nine sacks were found to be decayed, and the king ordered the mayor and bailiffs to allow the burgess to sell these, having given security that he would respond to the king for the money received.[47]

Exceptional responsibilities were given to the burgesses of Bristol and of Newcastle-on-Tyne. Those at Bristol were required to assume part of the responsibility for keeping as prisoner the king's cousin Eleanor, whose presence had necessitated some other services already noted. Two letters in 1224 ordered the bailiffs to associate four of the leading men of their town with themselves in a weekly inspection trip to the castle to make sure that Eleanor was being kept safely by royal officials there. Furthermore, the bailiffs and their associates were commanded to be present at a weekly accounting of the expenses for Eleanor and others in the castle held at the court of Radulphus de Wiliton' and to retain one roll from that accounting.[48]

Another unusual responsibility for burgesses is found in a letter of 1221 with the following salutation: "The mayor and reeves and all the burgesses of Newcastle-on-Tyne to all to whom these presents may come, greeting." The substance of

45. *Rot. Litt. Pat.*, p. 107a; *Rot. Litt. Cl.*, I, 121b, 123a; *C.R. 1227-31*, p. 271; *C.R. 1231-34*, pp. 358, 406, 414; *C.R. 1234-37*, pp. 120, 468; *C.R. 1242-47*, pp. 262, 264; *C.R. 1247-51*, p. 387; *C.R. 1251-53*, p. 248; *C.R. 1253-54*, p. 41.

46. *C.R. 1227-31*, pp. 142, 182; *C.R. 1234-37*, p. 393; *C.R. 1242-47*, p. 166.

47. *C.R. 1268-72*, p. 439.

48. *Rot. Litt. Cl.*, I, 624a, 649b.

the letter that follows is that the burgesses in a charter sealed with the common seal of the borough have pledged their properties and their bodies in behalf of Daniel, the son of Nicholas, to whom the king had committed the castle near their borough. However, this arrangement was of short duration, for two years later the king notified "his beloved and faithful Daniel of Newcastle and the other proved men of this same town" that he had committed the castle to William Brewer the younger, and ordered them to deliver it without delay.[49]

Clearly the kings felt free to call upon burgesses to act as their agents in almost any type of business, and this conclusion is strengthened by the variety of orders dispatched. In 1252 the mayor of Dunwich was ordered to associate a royal clerk with himself and four other men of the town for inquiring about goods of the hospital at Dunwich that had been taken into the king's hand, and to keep these goods safely and protect the clerk from violence while the seizure was being made.[50] Borough officials at Northampton had to proclaim that the owners must rebuild on vacant lots and seize into the king's hand any lots left vacant.[51] Even more unusual was the assignment of the mayor and sheriffs of London, who were directed to go in person along the Thames from London to the sea in order to burn all the fish-traps and small nets they could find, no matter in whose jurisdiction they were, and to remove all the weirs not anciently allowed.[52]

Royal protection for the Jews was made effective in the boroughs by orders from the king to borough officials. King John reminded the mayor and barons of London in a strongly-worded letter in 1203 that the Jews were under his special protection and notified them of his displeasure upon hearing that they had allowed harm to come to Jews in their city. He

49. *Pat. R.*, I, 367, 808.
51. *Ibid.*, p. 44.
50. *C.R. 1251-53*, p. 209.
52. *C.R. 1253-54*, p. 58.

noted that his stand was not taken for the sake of the Jews, but rather in behalf of the royal peace, "because if we had given our peace to a dog, it ought to be observed inviolate."[53] At Gloucester in 1218 the constable and reeves were ordered to free the Jews to the custody of twenty-four burgesses whose names were to be sent to the king and not to permit anyone, especially Crusaders, to molest the Jews in any way.[54] That same year a general order to several sheriffs and the citizens of York and Winchester directed them to protect the Jews, proclaim the king had given them his peace, and enforce the law that Jews could be brought to court only before the royal justices for custody of the Jews.[55] When the Jews complained to the king in 1222 that the archbishop of Canterbury and the bishop of Lincoln had issued statements to the effect that no one should sell foodstuffs to Jews, the king ordered the sheriff and mayor of Canterbury, the mayor and reeves of Oxford, and the bailiffs of Norwich to proclaim that food and other necessities were to be sold to Jews, and to arrest anyone who refused to do so.[56] Failure to take action after houses of Jews in Norwich had been set on fire brought a judgment against the bailiffs and the city in 1235.[57] Royal letters later in the century indicate protection for the Jews continued to be a problem for both the king and borough officials.[58]

Borough officials were sometimes called upon to make proclamations in the king's name on various subjects besides protection for the Jews. For example, the sheriffs of London were directed in 1212 to make known to all clerks and men of religion in their city that they were required to appear at court at a specified time.[59] In 1234 city officials at London were

53. *Rot. Litt. Pat.*, p. 33a.   54. *Rot. Litt. Cl.*, I, 354b.
55. *Pat. R.*, I, 157.   56. *Rot. Litt. Cl.*, I, 567a.
57. Richardson and Sayles, *Select Cases of Procedure without Writ*, p. 21.
58. *C.P.R. 1258-66*, p. 679; *C.P.R. 1272-81*, p. 157.
59. *Rot. Litt. Cl.*, I, 129b.

directed to proclaim that no law schools were to be permitted within the city.[60] Orders to proclaim the exemption from prize granted to men from Bordeaux in 1254 were sent to Southampton, Bristol, and Ipswich; city officials at Winchester were commanded earlier to proclaim that the king's prize would be taken four times a year.[61] In 1256 a royal letter ordered the officials of all the English cities and boroughs to proclaim a charter granted to the burgesses of St. Omer in Flanders.[62] After the baronial victory in the first part of the Barons' War in 1264, borough officials at Derby received orders to proclaim the king's peace.[63]

Even during the reign of John the burgesses had been called to send representatives for giving advice to the king and council upon specific problems and for receiving orders from the king and council in place of the whole borough. Usually the burgesses appeared in the capacity of experts, exemplified by the Londoners giving advice about new coinage or the men from the Cinque Ports helping make plans for coastal defense as discussed above in Chapters III and V respectively. Broader use of burgesses occurred when plans were made in 1223 to extend a truce with France, and information about any violations of the truce up to that time was obtained by ordering officials and some individuals in nine boroughs along the coast to let everyone in their jurisdictions know about the inquiry, discover any complaints, and appear at court prepared to respond to king and council on this question.[64] More opportunities for influencing decisions of the royal administration were forthcoming during the later thirteenth century, including the summons of borough representatives to parliament after 1265.

60. *C.R. 1234-37*, p. 26.
61. *C.P.R. 1232-47*, p. 238; *C.P.R. 1247-58*, p. 371.
62. *C.P.R. 1247-58*, p. 496.
63. *C.P.R. 1258-66*, p. 359.
64. *Rot. Litt. Cl.*, I, 629b.

Writs directed to the Cinque Ports in 1237, 1238, and 1242 ordered them to send men to discuss with royal officials certain business affecting the Ports and the royal administration.[65] In 1265 the Cinque Ports were ordered to send representatives to the king with full power to act in their behalf in making peace between the Ports and Yarmouth.[66] Writing about the assessment of a thirtieth in 1237, the Tewkesbury chronicler stated that it was done at a *magnum colloquium* and listed citizens and burgesses as present along with the magnates. The close roll writ, since it includes *milites et liberi homines,* who seem to have taken part in the proceedings, indicates that the chronicler may very well have been right in noting the presence of burgesses.[67] In 1254 the burgesses at Southampton were ordered to send their bailiff and twelve men to a meeting of the royal council to discuss the state of their town and other business to be expounded to them by the council.[68]

The parliament summoned by Simon de Montfort in 1265 was the first meeting where the boroughs were summoned for business stated in general terms, and where they were summoned along with barons and knights of the shire.[69] A fragment of council memoranda drawn up in 1268 for guidance of the chancellor in issuing writs under the great seal shows that twenty-seven selected towns were summoned before the council to treat of matters touching the king, the kingdom, and themselves.[70] The probable business at the meeting was the assess-

65. *C.P.R. 1232-47,* pp. 179, 209, 305.
66. *C.P.R. 1258-66,* p. 491.
67. Albert B. White, "Some Early Instances of Concentration of Representatives in England," *The American Historical Review,* XIX (1913-14), pp. 745-747.
68. *C.R. 1253-54,* p. 138.
69. *C.R. 1264-68,* pp. 87, 89, 112; May McKisack, *The Parliamentary Representation of the English Boroughs during the Middle Ages* (Oxford and London, 1932), p. 1.
70. Printed by G. O. Sayles, "Representation of Cities and Boroughs in 1268," *The English Historical Review,* XL (1925), pp. 580-585.

ment of a tallage.[71] Borough representatives were also present at the parliament of 1275 at which the wool trade was regulated for the first time.[72] Representatives from boroughs are also known to have been present at parliaments during the following years: 1283, 1295, 1296, 1298, 1300, 1301, 1302, 1305, 1306, and 1307.[73]

In 1303 representatives of forty-two towns were called to a colloquium of merchants in an effort to raise the rate of the custom on wool, but the burgesses stated, for themselves and their communities, that they would not consent to any increase in maletotes or customs, except the ancient debts and customs. As a result of this resistance, the project was dropped.[74] The mayor and five men of London were sent as representatives to the parliament in 1283 to consider the main item of business concerning how to deal with David son of Griffin, a Welsh rebel leader, and they were given the gruesome task of carrying the rebel's head back to the city, where it was placed on public view at the Tower.[75] Allowances from borough funds for the expenses of representatives to parliament have been found in the published borough records for Leicester, Norwich, and London.[76] Writs were dispatched to twenty-four boroughs in 1296 asking that two burgesses be chosen in each from those who would know best how to dispose and order a new town for the greatest advantage of the king and of merchants who would reside there or come there for business.[77] Writs for the expenses of the burgesses attending parliament were issued

71. Powicke, *Henry III and the Lord Edward*, II, 563.
72. C. Hilary Jenkinson, "The First Parliament of Edward I," *The English Historical Review*, XXV (1910), pp. 232, 236.
73. McKisack, pp. 6-11; Stubbs, *Select Charters*, pp. 458, 460-461, 478, 481-482, 496.
74. Stubbs, *Select Charters*, pp. 496-497.
75. Stubbs, *Chronicles of Edward I and Edward II*, I, 92 (*Annales Londoniensis*).
76. Mary Bateson, ed., *Records of the Borough of Leicester* (London, 1899), I, 235; Hudson and Tingey, *Records of Norwich*, II, 35; Sharpe, *Calendar of Letter-Books. Letter-Book B*, p. 215.
77. *C.C.R. 1288-96*, p. 515.

by the king in 1305 and 1307 and appear in the chancery rolls for those years.[78]

Without entering further into the complex question of the rise of parliament, that institution may be viewed from the standpoint of administration as an outgrowth of precedents both in the practice of consultation with burgesses and in financial negotiations with them. It is probably significant that nearly all the men who represented boroughs in the parliaments of the fourteenth century had had previous experience in the governments of their own boroughs.[79] Certainly it must have been no great change for such men accustomed to deal with royal orders in their official borough positions to assemble as a group in parliament, where similar royal business was presented. It was only later that parliament developed into a decision-making body with powers so far beyond those of borough officials carrying out royal administrative orders that the connection seems fanciful. Whatever else parliament may have been in 1307, it was an efficient means by which the royal administration was able to draw upon the services of the burgesses in England.

78. *C.C.R. 1302-07*, pp. 330, 524.
79. McKisack, p. 104; Sylvia L. Thrupp, *The Merchant Class of Medieval London* (Chicago, 1948), p. 57.

CHAPTER VIII. THE SIGNIFICANCE
OF THE BOROUGH IN ROYAL
ADMINISTRATION

THIRTEENTH-CENTURY writers often referred to the
borough as one of the "communities of the realm," using
a phrase that nicely conveys its status. Although an organization recognizable as having an identity of its own, the borough
did not develop in isolation, for the innovations of the Ange-
vins and the centralization effected by Edward I a century
later both had their effect. The king's need insured that the
limitation implied by the qualifying phrase "of the realm"
would not be overlooked, and that the borough would develop
in close connection with the monarchy at the administrative
center of that realm.

In fact, as a result both of the force of royal government
impinging upon the boroughs and the desire of the burgesses
for more privileges, the administrative functions had prolif-
erated, making the borough more important to the royal administration in 1307 than it had been in 1130. A study of
the records during this period carries one from a rather in-
formal, pragmatic use of the borough to an orderly system of

administration employing burgesses and their officials as an integral part of the operation. Yet it should be remembered that the essential precedents in the use of the borough, especially in managing the administrative work connected with the *firma burgi,* were present from the early evidence in the pipe rolls of the twelfth century, and needed only to be developed to reach the further potential realized by 1307.

Not much theorizing about the basis for royal authority over the boroughs was done in the thirteenth century, but the greater use of the borough for administrative purposes and scattered court decisions where the liberty of a borough had been claimed in disparagement of royal authority make it clear that the king's authority over the boroughs was real enough, whatever the theory may have been. The boroughs obtained more liberties throughout the period covered by this study, such as the *firma burgi* or the later *non-intromittant* and return of writs clauses, but with these liberties went responsibilities. The burgesses had to manage the details of finance in the first and had to bear the burden of administering justice with the latter privileges, undertaking duties that had previously been performed by the sheriff. Even though reliable performance of these duties was enforced by fines at the least, and a possible loss of liberties, the burgesses were anxious to get such clauses in their charters. The increased burden of responsibility was deemed preferable to being kept under the continued direct supervision of the sheriff. Certainly this was no sentimental regard for liberty on the part of the burgesses, but rather a realistic assessment involving the question of harassment by an unsympathetic official on the one hand and, on the other, the possibility of softening the effect of royal authority when the burgesses themselves made such authority effective.

A comparison of the administrative functions performed by

the burgesses and their officials with the functions of the sheriffs in the thirteenth century shows that the burgesses had superseded the sheriffs in nearly all their functions as far as the borough itself was concerned, and were paralleling and supplementing the work of the sheriffs in many other functions more general in scope. Functions of the sheriff emphasized by W. A. Morris in his definitive book on this official were the administration of justice, levy of taxation, collection of revenue, enforcement of military service, and summoning of local representatives to meet the king's justices.[1] Other functions in the order in which he discussed them were the custody of prisoners, various minor executive functions, regulation of commerce, making purchases and disbursements, supervision of the Jews, enforcement of coinage regulations, and proclaiming royal mandates.[2] In comparison, the discussion in the previous chapters has shown that by 1307 the burgesses were doing nearly all these same things for the king; with few exceptions they were being used in the same manner as sheriffs were used. It even appears that in one activity, the control and regulation of commerce, the burgesses were being used more than the sheriffs, judging from the contrast between the activity of the burgesses as previously discussed and the lack of emphasis on this aspect of the sheriff's work as described by Morris.

During the thirteenth century the power of the sheriff decreased to the point that the nature of the office itself was changed.

In the interval between the accession of Henry III. in 1216 and the death of his son Edward I. in 1307 the sheriff lost much of the semblance of immediate subordination to an absolute king. By the end of this period he appears, not so much the personal servant of the monarch, as the holder of an office the activities of which, in so far as they are controlled or directed by the chancery, the exchequer

1. *The Medieval English Sheriff to 1300* (Manchester, 1927), p. 111.
2. *Ibid.*, pp. 115, 117-118, 149, 154, 214, 216-217.

and the justices, are subjected in general to fixed rules and forms. The military functions in any proper sense of the word have vanished, the discretionary powers largely so, and the office once conferred upon the great officers of state, is usually held by members of local families who are in theory knights, and who sometimes bear the honorary title master.[3]

This decline of the sheriff is explained by the fact that many of his functions were taken over by newly created royal officials and by the expanding jurisdiction of the royal courts. It is somewhat less obvious, but nevertheless clear in the light of the administrative study of the boroughs, that exempting the boroughs from his jurisdiction was another means of limiting his office, and that other administrative tasks performed by burgesses in the same manner as sheriffs made that official no longer the indispensable support of the monarchy for dealing with local administration.

These tasks in which burgesses replaced the sheriff provide support for Albert B. White's thesis that the English people were trained in government as an incidental result of the policies of kings, who found it to their own advantage to use the people for various governmental tasks.[4] This training for burgesses took place in the practice of making allowances at the exchequer accounting, which had the effect of forcing borough officials to adopt some method for keeping a record of their expenses in carrying out the command in each royal letter and to follow some orderly procedure in carrying out such mandates. Further opportunity for learning better methods came in the administrative tasks performed jointly with royal clerks, who could draw upon the experience of the developing central administration. In another example, when security was taken from ship masters that they would not divert their cargoes from their stated ports of destination, officials of the port of depar-

3. *Ibid.*, p. 167.
4. *Self-Government at the King's Command*, p. 2 and *passim*.

ture must have made some record of the security taken and the conditions attached, and they also had to provide safe custody of any goods tendered as security. Borough officials where the cargo was discharged had to inspect it during the unloading to certify that the cargo had been delivered properly and the ship master was entitled to the return of his security. Other administrative orders required that reports of various types be sent to the central administration. These and other subsidiary activities involved in the execution of royal commands do not appear in the extant records, it is true, but they are implied, and added both to the burden imposed upon the burgesses or their officials and to the training in administration they absorbed.

However, these relationships and other examples that could be drawn from the previous chapters are purely administrative with little or no discretion allowed. It is questionable how much effect this sort of training had for self-government in any real sense. It was only in the areas of exempt jurisdiction, in finance and in justice, where no specific writs were issued that discretion involving the growth of a sense of responsibility in making decisions was allowed, and even in these areas there was a general supervision exercised by royal courts. The burgesses on rare occasions were consulted by the king, usually in the status of expert witnesses, and had some chance to influence the making of decisions. Their presence in parliament later may have given occasional opportunities for at least stating their views, if not wielding influence over decisions, and a few examples involving taxes and customs indicate these views had some effect. Nevertheless, the administrative activities of the English burgess prior to 1307 were narrowly conceived, and White's thesis, illuminating as it is, can easily be given more emphasis than the facts warrant.

When the administrative functions of the borough are considered as a whole, certain developments stand out that may have been somewhat obscured by the rather arbitrary classifications imposed upon the evidence for the sake of orderly discussion. In all areas dealing with finance and commerce, use of the borough was especially important. Boroughs served as points of contact bringing the king into touch with the non-agrarian part of the English economy in administering customs regulations, making disbursements, enforcing coinage regulations, providing military supplies, controlling shipping, and purveying items at the royal command. In a period in which royal finances were undependable and rather inflexible by nature, use of the borough was of real importance in meeting the needs of the monarchy. Not that the use of boroughs in these ways gave the royal administration any rigid control over this part of the economy, but it did give the means by which the king could intervene to establish temporary control or supply his needs.

More indirect testimony to the significance of the borough in royal administration is given by the references to events that reflect the history of the time, providing the detailed evidence to show how larger decisions were put into practice by the day-to-day working of the royal administration. Although great events cast a shadow in this mass of administrative detail, both famous and obscure personalities find their way into the records in a truly egalitarian fashion. The principals in all this activity are the anonymous borough officials and the burgesses themselves, but they are observed only in fleeting glimpses hidden behind references to the tasks they performed in royal administration.

Moreover, the status of a particular borough was of little importance to its administrative use. Whether borough officials were elective or royal appointees, whether the borough was rich and powerful or not, the king's authority was superior, and all alike served him in an administrative capacity. Borough officials served in conjunction with sheriffs and other royal officials, sometimes even inspecting their work for the king, but in other tasks burgesses served alongside men without liberties from the royal manors.[5] Even the growth in efficiency of the royal administration by 1307 did not replace the use of boroughs with royal officials, but drew the borough increasingly into that administration. By issuing a chancery writ, the king and his officials could call upon the services of any borough throughout England. Convenience and usage provide the explanation of this policy by which the crown came to treat the borough and its officials as an integral part of royal administration during the twelfth and thirteenth centuries.

5. This lack of differentiation is vividly illustrated by payments to royal messengers whose deliveries included all these types. See *Liber Quotidianus Contratularis Garderobae,* p. 284.

APPENDIX. POSSESSION OF THE *FIRMA BURGI*

This chart showing possession of the *firma burgi* with some indication of the source is intended to justify the selection of borough accounts used for this book and to take the place of a discussion in Chapter III of the *firma burgi* after the time of Henry II. Pipe roll references given in this chart for the reigns of Richard I and John show the first appearance of a new grant of *firma burgi* on the pipe rolls; those for Henry III only relate to the years for which the pipe rolls have been published.

		P.R. 14 Hen. III	P.R. 26 Hen. III
Andover	1201*	X	X
Appleby	1200*		
Bamburgh	1257 (*P.R. 41 Hen. III in* Hodgson, *Northumberland*)		
Bedford	1189**	X	X
Bridgnorth	1176 to 1189**; 1190 (*P.R. 2 Ric. I*) and after	X	X
Bristol	1224 (*P.R. 8 Hen. III* in Madox, *Exchequer,* I, 334 n.)		
Cambridge	1185* to 1189**; 1207 and after*	X	X
Canterbury	1201 (*P.R. 3 John*); 1234*		
Carlisle	1221*		
Chichester	1226 (deduced from *P.R. 14 Hen. III*)		
Colchester	1188 reeves as royal offs.**; 1189 and after**	X	X
Derby	1204*	X	X
Dunwich	1200* and 1205*	X	X
Exeter	1259*		
Gloucester	1165 to 1176**; 1194* (*P.R. 8 Ric. I*); 1200*		X

		P.R. 14 Hen. III	P.R. 26 Hen. III
Grimsby	1160-61 only**; 1196 (*P.R. 8 John*); 1227*		
Hereford	1189*; 1215*		X
Huntingdon	1205*	X	X
Ilchester	1204*		X
Ipswich	1194 (*P.R. 6 Ric I*)	X	X
Kingston-on-Thames	1208*		X
Lancaster		X	
Lincoln	1130 to 1157**; 1162 to 1190**; 1194* and after	X	X
London	1131*; 1190**; 1194**; 1199* and after	X	X
Newcastle-on-Tyne	1201*	X	X
Northampton	1184-85 to 1189**; 1189*	X	X
Norwich	1194*	X	X
Nottingham	1189**	X	X
Orford	1194 (*P.R. 6 Ric. I*); 1256*		
Oxford	1199*		
Portsmouth	1229*	X	X
Rochester	1192 (*P.R. 4 Ric. I*); 1227*	X	X
Scarborough	1201*	X	X
Shrewsbury	1175-76** to 1189* (*P.R. 2 Ric. I*) and after	X	X
Southampton	1166 to 1189 by reeves**; 1189 reeve (*P.R. 1 Ric. I*) to 1190 (*P.R. 2 Ric. I*); 1199*	X	X
Stafford	1206**		
Wallingford	1155** to 1182**; 1189 and after (deduced from *P.R. 4 Ric. I*)		
Winchester	1199 (*P.R. 1 John*)		
Worcester	1189*	X	X
Yarmouth	1208*	X	
York	1190**	X	X

* Based on a charter included in Ballard and Tait, *British Borough Charters*, I-II.
** Date given in Tait, *Medieval Borough* in his essay on *firma burgi*, pp. 154-183.

BIBLIOGRAPHY

I. SOURCES

A. *Exchequer and Chancery Records*

Calendar of Inquisitions Miscellaneous (Chancery). Vol. I, 1219-1307. London, 1916.

Calendar of the Close Rolls 1272-1307. 5 vols. The Deputy Keeper of the Records. London, 1900-1908.

Calendar of the Fine Rolls. Vol. I, 1272-1307. London, 1911.

Calendar of the Liberate Rolls 1227-1260. 4 vols. The Deputy Keeper of the Records. London, 1916-59.

Calendar of the Patent Rolls 1232-1307. 8 vols. The Deputy Keeper of the Records. London, 1893-1913.

Cannon, Henry L., ed. *The Great Roll of the Pipe for the Twenty-Sixth Year of the Reign of King Henry the Third A.D. 1241-42.* New Haven and London, 1918.

Close Rolls 1227-1272. 14 vols. The Deputy Keeper of the Records. London, 1902-38.

Eyton, R. W., ed. *The Staffordshire Pipe Rolls, of the Reigns of King Richard I and King John, A.D. 1189 to A.D. 1216.* Collections for a History of Staffordshire. The William Salt Archaeological Society, II. Birmingham, 1881.

Hodgson, John. *A History of Northumberland.* 3 parts, 7 vols. Newcastle-Upon-Tyne, 1820-58. Part III, vol. 3 contains the Northumberland entries on the pipe rolls from 13 John to 56 Henry III.

Hunter, Joseph, ed. *The Great Roll of the Pipe for the First Year of Richard the First, A.D. 1189-1190.* Record Commission. London, 1844.

The Great Rolls of the Pipe for the Second, Third, and Fourth Years of the Reign of King Henry the Second. Facsimile of the 1844 Record Commission ed. London, 1930.

Magnum Rotulum Scaccarii, vel Magnum Rotulum Pipae de Anno

Tricesimo-primo Regni Henrici Primi. Facsimile of the 1833 Record Commission ed. London, 1929.

Jenkinson, Hilary, and E. R. F. Beryl, eds. *Select Cases in the Exchequer of Pleas.* Selden Society, XLVIII. London, 1932.

The Memoranda Roll for . . . the First Year of King John (1199-1200). Pipe Roll Society, New Series, XXI. London, 1943.

The Memoranda Roll for the Tenth Year of the Reign of King John (1207-8). Ed. R. Allen Brown. Pipe Roll Society, New Series, LXIX. London, 1957.

The Memoranda Roll of the King's Remembrancer for Michaelmas 1230-Trinity 1231. Ed. Chalfant Robinson. Pipe Roll Society, New Series XI. Princeton, 1933.

Michel, Francisque, ed. *Rôles gascons.* Vol. I. Collection de documents inédits sur l'histoire de France. Paris, 1885. Contains the *liberate* rolls for 26 Henry III.

Mills, M. H., ed. *The Pipe Roll for 1295 Surrey Membrane.* Surrey Record Society, VIII. Guildford and Esher, 1924.

Mills, Mabel, and R. Stewart-Brown, eds. *Cheshire in the Pipe Rolls 1158-1301.* The Record Society for the Publication of Original Documents Relating to Lancashire and Cheshire, XCII. [n.p.] 1938.

Parker, F. H. M., ed. *The Pipe Rolls of Cumberland and Westmorland 1222-1260.* Cumberland and Westmorland Antiquarian and Archaeological Society. Extra Series, XII. Kendal, 1905.

Patent Rolls 1216-1232. 2 vols. The Deputy Keeper of the Records. London, 1901-3.

Pipe Roll Society. *The Great Roll of the Pipe* [1158-89; 1190-1212; 1230] 53 vols. Original series, 1-38. New series, 1-30. London, 1884-1955.

Rotuli de Liberate ac de Misis et Praestitis, Regnante Johanne. Ed. T. Duffus Hardy. Record Commission. London, 1844.

Rotuli Litterarum Clausarum. Ed. Thomas D. Hardy. 2 vols. Record Commission. London, 1833-44.

Rotuli Litterarum Patentium. Ed. Thomas D. Hardy. Only vol. I, part 1 published. Record Commission. London, 1835.

Rotuli Originalium in Curia Scaccarii Abbreviatio. Vol. I. Record Commission. London, 1805.

B. *Other Sources*

Baildon, William P., ed. *Select Civil Pleas.* Selden Society, III. London, 1890.

Bain, Joseph, ed. *Calendar of Documents Relating to Scotland.* Vol. II only. Edinburgh, 1884.

Ballard, Adolphus, *et al.*, eds. *British Borough Charters 1042-1660*. 3 vols. Cambridge, 1913-43. Vol. II, 1216-1307, ed. James Tait.

Bateson, Mary, ed. *Borough Customs*. 2 vols. Selden Society, Vols. XVIII and XXII. London, 1904-6.

Records of the Borough of Leicester. Vol. I, 1103-1327, London, 1899.

Bracton, Henricus de. *De Legibus et Consuetudinibus Angliae*. Ed. George E. Woodbine. 4 vols. New Haven, 1915-42.

Croniques de London depuis l'an 44 Hen. III jusqu'à l'an 17 Edw. III. Ed. George James Aungier. Camden Society, No. XXVIII. London, 1844.

Curia Regis Rolls. 12 vols. London, 1922-57.

De Antiquis Legibus Liber. Cronica Maiorum et Vicecomitum Londoninarum. Ed. Thomas Stapleton. Camden Society, No. XXXIV. London, 1846.

Fitz-Nigel, Richard. *Dialogus de Scaccario. De Necessariis Observantiis Scaccario*. Ed. Arthur Hughes, C. G. Crump, and C. Johnson. Oxford, 1902.

The Course of the Exchequer. Text and translation by Charles Johnson. New York, 1950.

Fleta. Only Vol. II published. Ed. H. G. Richardson and G. O. Sayles. Selden Society, LXXII. London, 1955.

Gervase of Canterbury. *The Historical Works of Gervase of Canterbury*. Vol. II *Gesta Regum*. Ed. William Stubbs. Rolls Series. London, 1880.

Gross, Charles, ed. *Select Cases from the Coroners' Rolls A.D. 1265-1413*. Selden Society, IX. London, 1896.

Hopkins, A., ed. *Selected Rolls of the Chester City Courts*. Chetham Society, 3rd ser., II. Manchester, 1950.

Hudson, William and John C. Tingey, eds. *The Records of the City of Norwich*. 2 vols. Norwich and London, 1906-10.

Leadam, I. S. and J. F. Baldwin, *Select Cases before the King's Council 1243-1482*. Selden Society, XXXV. Cambridge, Mass., 1918.

Liber Quotidianus Contrarotulatoris Garderobae. Anno Regis Edwardi Vicesimo Octavo. Ed. John Topham. London, 1787.

Maitland, F. W. *Bracton's Note Book*. 3 vols. London, 1887.

Select Pleas of the Crown. Selden Society, I. London, 1888.

Placita de Quo Warranto. Record Commission. London, 1818.

Placitorum in Domo Capitulari Westmonasteriensi Asservatorum Abbreviatio. Record Commission. London, 1811.

Richardson, H. G., and G. O. Sayles, eds. *Select Cases of Procedure without Writ under Henry III*. Selden Society, LX. London, 1941.

Riley, Henry T., trans. *Chronicles of the Mayors and Sheriffs of London, A.D. 1188 to A.D. 1274. The French Chronicle of London, A.D. 1259 to A.D. 1343.* London, 1863.

Munimenta Gildhallae Londoniensis. Vol. II, Parts 1-2 *Liber Custumarum.* Rolls Series. London, 1860.

Rogers, J. E. Thorold, ed. *Oxford City Documents Financial and Judicial 1268-1665.* Oxford Historical Society, XVIII. Oxford, 1891.

Rotuli Hundredorum. 2 vols. Record Commission. London, 1812-18.

Rymer, Thomas, ed. *Foedera, Conventiones, Litterae et Cujuscunque Generis Acta Publica.* Revised by Adam Clarke and Fred. Holbrooke. Vol. I. Record Commission. London, 1816.

Salter, Rev. H. E., ed. *Munimenta Civitatis Oxonie.* Oxford Historical Society, LXXI. Devizes, 1920.

Sayles, G. O. *Select Cases in the Court of King's Bench under Edward I.* 3 vols. Selden Society, LV, LVII, LVIII. London, 1936-39.

Sharpe, Reginald R., ed. *Calendar of Letter-Books Preserved among the Archives . . . of the City of London at the Guildhall.*

Letter-Book A. Circa A.D. 1275-1298. London, 1899.

Letter-Book B. Circa A.D. 1275-1312. London, 1900.

Letter-Book C. Circa A.D. 1291-1309. London, 1901.

Shirley, Walter W., ed. *Royal and Other Historical Letters Illustrative of the Reign of Henry III.* 2 vols. Rolls Series. London, 1862-66.

The Statutes of the Realm. Vol. I. Record Commission. London, 1810.

Stenton, Doris Mary, ed. *The Earliest Lincolnshire Assize Rolls A.D. 1202-1209.* Lincoln Record Society, XXII. n.p., 1926.

The Earliest Northamptonshire Assize Rolls A.D. 1202 and 1203. Northamptonshire Record Society, V. Lincoln and London, 1930.

Pleas before the King or His Justices 1198-1202. 2 vols. Selden Society, LXVII, LXVIII. London, 1952-53.

Rolls of the Justices in Eyre. Being the Rolls of Pleas and Assizes for Gloucestershire, Warwickshire and Staffordshire, 1221, 1222. Selden Society, LIX. London, 1940.

Rolls of the Justices in Eyre Being the Rolls of Pleas and Assizes for Lincolnshire 1218-9 and Worcestershire 1221. Selden Society, LIII. London, 1934.

Rolls of the Justices in Eyre Being the Rolls of Pleas and Assizes for Lincolnshire 1218-9 and Worcestershire 1221. Selden Society, London, 1937.

Stewart-Brown, R. *Calendar of County Court, City Court and Eyre Rolls of Chester, 1259-1297.* Chetham Society, new series 84. Manchester, 1925.

Stubbs, William, ed. *Chronicles of the Reigns of Edward I and Edward II*. Vol. I *Annales Londoniensis*. Rolls Series. London, 1882.
Select Charters and Other Illustrations of English Constitutional History. 9th ed. rev. by H. W. C. Davis. Oxford, 1913.

Thomas, A. H. *Calendar of Early Mayor's Court Rolls . . . A.D. 1298-1307*. Cambridge, 1924.

Year Books of the Reign of King Edward the First [Years 20-22; 30-35]. Ed. Alfred J. Horwood. 5 vols. Rolls Series. London, 1866-79.

II. SECONDARY WORKS

Ballard, Adolphus. *The English Borough in the Twelfth Century*. Cambridge, 1914.

Brooks, F. W. *The English Naval Forces 1199-1272*. London, [1932].
"William de Wrotham and the Office of Keeper of the King's Ports and Galleys," *The English Historical Review*, XL (1925), 570-579.

Chrimes, S. B. *An Introduction to the Administrative History of Mediaeval England*. Oxford, 1952.

Galbraith, V. H. *An Introduction to the Use of Public Records*. Oxford, 1934.

Giuseppi, M. S. *A Guide to the Manuscripts Preserved in the Public Record Office*. 2 vols. London, 1923-24.

Gras, Norman S. B. *The Early English Customs System*. Harvard Economic Studies, XVIII. Cambridge, Mass., 1918.

Gross, Charles. *A Bibliography of British Municipal History*. Harvard Historical Studies, V. New York, 1897.
The Gild Merchant. 2 vols. Oxford, 1890.

Hardy, Thomas Duffus. *Syllabus (in English) of the Documents . . . contained in the Collection Known as "Rymer's Foedera."* 3 vols. London, 1869-85.

Hill, J. W. F. *Medieval Lincoln*. Cambridge, 1948.

Jenkinson, C. Hilary. "The First Parliament of Edward I:" *The English Historical Review*, XXV (1910), 231-242.

Jolliffe, J. E. A. *Angevin Kingship*. New York, 1955.
The Constitutional History of Medieval England. London, 1937.

Little, Bryan. *The City and County of Bristol*. London, 1954.

McKisack, May. *The Parliamentary Representation of the English Boroughs during the Middle Ages*. Oxford and London, 1932.

Madox, Thomas. *Firma Burgi, or an Historical Essay Concerning the Cities Towns and Buroughs of England*. London, 1726.

The History and Antiquities of the Exchequer. 2 vols. London, 1769.

Maitland, Frederic William. *Township and Borough.* Cambridge, 1898.

Meyer, Erwin F. "Boroughs," in James F. Willard *et al. The English Government at Work, 1327-1336.* 3 vols. Cambridge, 1940-50.

"Some Aspects of *Withernam* or the English Mediaeval System of Vicarious Liability," *Speculum,* VIII (1933), 235-240.

Mitchell, Sydney K. *Studies in Taxation under John and Henry III.* New Haven and London, 1914.

Taxation in Medieval England. Ed. Sidney Painter. Yale Historical Publications, Studies XV. New Haven, 1951.

Morris, John E. *The Welsh Wars of Edward I.* Oxford, 1901.

Morris, William A. *The Medieval English Sheriff to 1300.* Manchester, 1927.

Murray, K. M. E. *The Constitutional History of the Cinque Ports.* Manchester, 1935.

Pollock, Sir Frederick, and Frederic William Maitland. *The History of English Law before the Time of Edward I.* 2nd ed. 2 vols. Cambridge, 1923.

Poole, Austin Lane. *From Domesday Book to Magna Carta 1087-1216.* The Oxford History of England. Oxford, 1951.

Poole, Reginald L. *The Exchequer in the Twelfth Century.* Oxford, 1912.

Powicke, F. M. *King Henry III and the Lord Edward.* 2 vols. Oxford, 1947.

Powicke, Sir Maurice. *The Thirteenth Century 1216-1307.* The Oxford History of England. Oxford, 1953.

Sayles, G. O. "Representation of Cities and Boroughs in 1268," *The English Historical Review,* XL (1925), 580-585.

Stephenson, Carl. "The Aids of the English Boroughs," *The English Historical Review,* XXXIV (1919), 457-475.

Borough and Town. Cambridge, Mass., 1933.

Stubbs, William. *The Constitutional History of England.* 5th ed. 3 vols. Oxford, 1891-96.

Sturler, Jean de. *Les relations politiques et les échanges commerciaux entre le duché de Brabant et l'Angleterre au moyen âge.* Paris, 1936.

Tait, James. *The Medieval English Borough.* Manchester, 1936.

Thrupp, Sylvia L. *The Merchant Class of Medieval London.* Chicago, 1948.

Tout, T. F. *Chapters in the Administrative History of Mediaeval England.* 6 vols. Manchester, 1920-33.

White, Albert B. *Self-Government at the King's Command: A Study in the Beginnings of English Democracy.* Minneapolis, 1933.

"Some Early Instances of Concentration of Representatives in England," *The American Historical Review,* XIX (1913-14), 735-750.

Wilkinson, B. *The Constitutional History of England 1216-1399.* 3 vols. London, Toronto, and N. Y., 1948-58.

The Mediaeval Council of Exeter. Manchester, 1931.

Willard, James F. *Parliamentary Taxes on Personal Property 1290 to 1334.* Cambridge, Mass., 1934.

INDEX